Warrior Queen:
Answering the Call of The Morrigan

a Girl God Anthology

Edited by Trista Hendren,
Jessica Johnson
and Pat Daly

Preface by Joey Morris

Cover Art by Arna Baartz

©2021 All Rights Reserved

ISBN: 978-82-93725-10-7

www.thegirlgod.com

Girl God Books

Original Resistance: Reclaiming Lilith, Reclaiming Ourselves
There is, perhaps, no more powerful archetype of female resistance than Lilith. As women across the globe rise up against the patriarchy, Lilith stands beside them, misogyny's original challenger. This anthology—a chorus of voices hitting chords of defiance, liberation, anger and joy—reclaims the goodness of women bold enough to hold tight to their essence. Through poetry, prose, incantation, prayer and imagery, women from all walks of life invite you to join them in the revolutionary act of claiming their place—of reclaiming themselves.

Re-visioning Medusa: from Monster to Divine Wisdom
A remarkable collection of essays, poems, and art by scholars who have researched Her, artists who have envisioned Her, and women who have known Her in their personal story. All have spoken with Her and share something of their communion in this anthology.

Inanna's Ascent: Reclaiming Female Power
Inanna's Ascent examines how females can rise from the underworld and reclaim their power, sovereignly expressed through poetry, prose and visual art. All contributors are extraordinary women in their own right, who have been through some difficult life lessons—and are brave enough to share their stories.

On the Wings of Isis: Reclaiming the Sovereignty of Auset
For centuries, women have lived, fought and died for their equality, independence and sovereignty. Originally known as Auset, the Egyptian Goddess Isis reveals such a path. Unfurl your wings and join an array of strong women who have embodied the Goddess of Ten Thousand Names to celebrate their authentic selves.

New Love: a reprogramming toolbox for undoing the knots

A powerful combination of emotional/spiritual techniques, art and inspiring words for women who wish to move away from patriarchal thought. *New Love* includes a mixture of compelling thoughts and suggestions for each day, along with a "toolbox" to help you change the parts of your life you want to heal.

Hearts Aren't Made of Glass

My Journey from Princess of Nothing to Goddess of My Own Damned Life—a memoir of sorts by Trista Hendren.

How to Live Well Despite Capitalist Patriarchy

A book challenging societal assumptions to help women become stronger and break free of their chains.

The Girl God

A book for children young and old, celebrating the Divine Female by Trista Hendren. Magically illustrated by Elisabeth Slettnes with quotes from various faith traditions and feminist thinkers.

Tell Me Why

A feminist twist of the creation story told with love from a mother to her son, in hopes of crafting a different world for them both. Written by Trista Hendren / Illustrated by Elisabeth Slettnes.

My Name is Medusa

The story of the greatly misunderstood Goddess, including why she likes snakes. *My Name is Medusa* explores the "scary" dark side, the potency of nature and the importance of dreams. Arna Baartz gorgeously illustrates this tale by Glenys Livingstone, teaching children (big and small) that our power often lies in what we have been taught to fear and revile.

My Name is Inanna

Tamara Albanna weaves the tale of Inanna's despair, strength and triumph—giving children of all ages hope that the dark times in life will pass. Arna Baartz illustrates this journey with gorgeous paintings of the owls, lions, stars, sun and moon that direct Her. *My Name is Inanna* is dedicated to Tamara's beloved homeland, Iraq—The Cradle of Civilization; the Land of the Goddess.

My Name is Lilith

Whether you are familiar with the legend of Lilith or hearing it for the first time, you will be carried away by this lavishly illustrated tale of the world's first woman. This creative retelling of Lilith's role in humanity's origins will empower girls and boys to seek relationships based on equality rather than hierarchy.

My Name is Isis

In this fresh look at the ancient Egyptian Goddess, Susan Morgaine reclaims Isis as The Great Mother Goddess and The Giver of Life, from whom all things come. Arna Baartz mystically illustrates Her as healer and protectress.

My Name is The Morrigan

The Morrigan remains one of the most misunderstood goddesses of the Celtic pantheon. Her mythology is a tangled web of various guises, deeds, and battles—and even her name is a bit of a mystery! Dive into the world of the Goddess of Death, and learn about what The Morrigan really has to teach us—and, maybe you'll find that She, and death, aren't so scary after all!

My Name is Goddess of Willendorf

Today more than ever, the image of the Goddess of Willendorf is a relevant one. Women and girls are bombarded with Photoshopped images of an "ideal" body shape that is quite literally unattainable. Remembering Willendorf's powerful story reminds us of the beautiful abundance of the female body, with all of her hills and valleys, lush softness, and fertility. You don't want to miss this body-positive celebration of the Great Mother Goddess!

Complete list of Girl God publications at www.thegirlgod.com

"Within the war we are all waging with the forces of death, subtle and otherwise, conscious or not – I am not only a casualty, I am also a warrior."
–Audre Lorde

Table of Contents

Preface   1
Joey Morris

Introduction   4
Jessica Johnson

A Note About Styles, Preferences and Language   6
Trista Hendren

Casting the Circle of The Great Queen   9
Nikki Wardwell Sleath

The Great Queen   11
Andrea Redmond

Painted In Blood & Woad   12
Phoenix Angelis

Call of The Morrigan   13
Jessica Johnson

The Morrigan   19
Lisbeth Cheever-Gessaman

When the Warrior Doesn't Win   20
Barbara Whiterose Marie McSweeney PhD

Macha's Curse   27
Stephanie Woodfield

Crow Woman: Morrigan of Sacred Wrath   28
Iriome R. Martín Alonso

Morrigan, Mother of Sacred Wrath: 29
Why Being Angry is Necessary
Iriome R. Martín Alonso

Woman of Fire and Solar Alchemy: 37
My Personal Vision of The Morrighan
Arlene Bailey

Magic and Mystery: Answering Her Call 39
Arlene Bailey

The Morrighan Speaks 40
Arlene Bailey

Crow Guardian 44
Arna Baartz

Birth of War 45
Jaclyn Cherie

Morrigan and Her Crows 52
Paul Nixon

Where You're Supposed to Be 53
Molly Remer

A Shriek Goddessy 55
Claire Dorey

Fox Goddess 65
Alissa DeLaFuente

Offering 66
Alissa DeLaFuente

Raven 67
Alissa DeLaFuente

Answering The Morrigan's Call: 68
Walking Beneath the Raven's Eye
Karen Storminger

A Blessing for the Brave and Tender   74
Molly Remer

The Hunter   75
Andrea Redmond

The Shining Ones   76
Molly Remer

Birth, Death and Rebirth—   77
How The Morrigan Restored My Sovereignty
A personal essay by Dr Karen Ward

Rise of The Morrigan   80
Paul Nixon

A Seed Dream   81
Molly Remer

Sometimes   82
Jessica Johnson

Morrigan   85
Laura Cameron

Finding the Strength to Love and   86
Re-Claiming My Sovereignty
Deborah A. Meyerriecks

Ravenspirit   93
Laura Cameron

Badass Warrior Goddess   94
Sharon Smith

The Morrigan Mask   97
Lauren Raine

Eel Kundalini, St Patriarch   98
and the Wide Sargasso Sea
Claire Dorey

I am The Morrigan   108
Kat Shaw

How to Make a GladiatHER   110
Bek Paroz

Beyond Their Eyes   116
Rosanna Maria Maher

She's Always Been With Me   117
Kerry Purdy

A Pagan Prayer to the Raven   126
Nicola O'Hanlon

Sovereignty Under The Morrigan   127
Joey Morris

On the Wing of Morrigan   130
Barbara O' Meara

The Vigil   131
Arlene Bailey

Awaken the Morrighan   133
Arlene Bailey

My Morrigan Story   134
Sam (Bo) Thompson

My Morrigan   140
Ashley McCormack

Channeled
Rosanna Maria Maher

141

The Price of Answering her Call
Sionainn McLean

142

My Name is The Morrigan
Arna Baartz

146

Calling in the Morrigan
Teresa Hess

147

Darkarma
Sharon Smith

151

Morrigan II
Laura Cameron

153

The Raven and the Wren
Erika Lopp

154

The Young Sovereign
Andrea Redmond

157

Mysteries of the Dark
Kay Turner

158

Sword at my Back
Karen Storminger

160

Strength in Softening
Jessica Johnson

161

A Reckoning with The Morrigan
Iris Eve

165

Mór Ríoghain – A Corvid Vision
Iyana Rashil

167

I Inherit Your Name, Morrigan 175
Mary Ellen Talley

Becoming Morrigan 177
Barbara O' Meara

My Final Offering 178
Raya Elyse Bencivenga

From Go to Goddess 179
Alyssa Spungen

The Washer at the Ford 187
Lauren Hershey

The Curse of The Morrigan 189
Lauren Raine

Samhain Eve at the River 191
H. Byron Ballard

War Crow Mixed Media Statue 195
Molly Roberts

The Morrigan Speaks 198
The Reclamation
Molly Remer

I am the Morrigan 200
Barbara O' Meara

Warrior Queen Wake-Up Call 201
Trista Hendren

List of Contributors 208

Acknowledgments 226

Preface

Joey Morris

Anger is at the roots, inviting a kind of war.

It burns and bubbles there, wrathful, terrible and necessary, daring to break the chains of apathetic thinking.

It is the combustive element that lights a spark amongst the gunpowder, until all the rotten foundations are burning, breaking under their outdated weight, and with a snap of reckoning, change is ushered in: the whole prison comes tumbling down.

Beyond the Morrigan's anger there are only ashes; remnants of what once was that did not serve and so met its end.

Here she extends a soot-stained hand inviting you to mark your face ready for battle, to grit your teeth through the thin veneer of the extinct that lines them, to cry out for justice and change, to howl and gnash in defiance.

We live in a world where it is fashionable to be well-liked, beautiful in your softness, appeasing and compliant.

Simply smile and carry on. Don't make waves. Speak softly and flash your flesh. Make them like you.

But the Morrigan was never one for platitudes.

She is the overstretched jaw screaming for bloody justice, mouth tearing at the cheeks beyond the level of comfort, her teeth bared wide, sharp, and menacing.

Muscular and limber, ready to crush skulls, or a phantom displaying all the discomforts of Death, like a veil stretched over a rotten corpse.

All depending on Her mood, of course, She never was one for standing still, or fulfilling expectation. Describing her aesthetic is like grabbing at water.

Her anger is deep and dangerous, shifting the narrative of entire worlds with a countenance designed for dread... your comfort level is not required.

You grow in pain.

Morrigan trucks in blood, and pain, and death, and prophecy.

You cannot live in anger, not always, because you become senseless and blind—but without it, you become a cold shell of yourself, disastrous in your neglect of self. Laying down to die, because all the fight has drained. And The Morrigan guards your death, tailor-picked by Her bloody hand, knowing ahead of time where and when you will fall. It belongs to Her and inviting otherwise incites a simmering rage.

To court such emptiness, to give up the ghost, to forget everything that should matter... is not acceptable.

And so She stands crooked on one left limb, screeching insults to get a rise, to torment you into action, any action, as long as you move.

And you will move.

Trust and believe.

When the Morrigan calls to us, it will be in the hardest times of our lives, when we are wracked with pain, fear, guilt, or languish into despondency or apathy.

It takes courage to answer Her, and stay by her side, as She forges you anew from the fires of your hurt, your anguish... and so I honour all of those within these pages for their bravery, their honesty, and their integrity in speaking of their experiences. And to Jess, a glorious warrior and dear friend.

Hail to the Morrigan
Mother to my Glory
Mother of my story
The bloody
And
The Gory
Speak all who died before me
'Memento Mori'
Hail to the Morrigan

Introduction

Jessica Johnson

Over the past year, I've been slowly gathering stories, poems, chants, songs, and rituals about The Morrigan from people all over the world. This powerful Irish goddess has had quite the reputation over the years as being vengeful and problematic to work with, and I knew when I began my path with her that it wasn't always going to be easy. But reading the words and seeing the art that has been created in her name, seeing the different ways that The Morrigan has moved people to create, has shown me proof many times over that she isn't the scary warrior that people paint her to be. Those who work closely with The Morrigan know she can be ruthless when she needs to be, but that this is always a last resort. Why then, do pagans continue to paint her in this dangerous light?

For the same reason that anyone who doesn't worship God and go to church gets called a devil-worshiper, or people do a double-take whenever they see a woman wearing a hijab or niqab. They fear what they do not understand, and they fear things that make them uncomfortable. The Morrigan is a goddess who makes you face your shadows and your inner demons, and she doesn't let you get away with avoiding the work for very long. She puts you through your paces and doesn't let you ignore what's important. She knows that our human life is precious, that we are not always guaranteed a long and comfortable life, and that we'll be better versions of ourselves if we face these issues, heal them, and grow from the experience. The Morrigan is a mother goddess too, she is not just a fearsome crow, flying over the battlefield, feasting on the fallen. She is a prophetess, a mighty worker of magick, and a loving, caring mother who takes steps to protect her own.

If you too have been called by The Morrigan, then let this book be a primer, a guide to what life might be like working with her, and doing her work and being in her service. Because that's what working with any deity actually is, being in service to them. Your service might look like mine, teaching people about her, writing about her guises and my personal understanding of her, and making it easier for others to take up her work. Or, it could look like providing services to veterans and people who have actually been through real war, and are trying to deal with the trauma of what they've been through. It could be providing priest or priestess duties to the community, or even working in activism to bring human rights to marginalized groups of people, animals, or protection for the environment. Whatever your service looks like, it's exactly right for you and her purposes for you.

Just like any god or goddess shrouded in mystery, The Morrigan's community is vast and varied, and experiences its fair number of challenges. Whenever you get a bunch of people together to celebrate a goddess of war, you are bound to see some tempers flare. But within the pages of this book, you will find no gatekeeping. You will find no racism, sexism, or bigotry. Within this community of children of The Morrigan, we welcome anyone who is called to work with her, regardless of skin tone, religion, sexuality, or gender. We welcome you into the circle, and we want to share what we have experienced of her with you. You may find that there are days when you feel like you just can't keep doing the work she has laid at your feet, and those are the days I recommend you pick this book back up and peruse the pages and find your motivation to keep going. Within these pages is support, understanding, and stories of people who kept going, or who were remade through working with her. Within these pages, you are welcome, you are seen, you are safe, and you belong. So come, sit down, get yourself a comforting beverage of choice, and sit with us. We have so much we want to share with you.

A Note on Styles, Preferences and Language
Trista Hendren

Warrior Queen contains a variety of writing styles from people around the world. Various forms of English are included in this anthology and we chose to keep spellings of the writers' place of origin to honor/honour each individual's unique voice.

It was the expressed intent of the editors to not police standards of citation, transliteration and formatting. Contributors have determined which citation style, italicization policy and transliteration system to adopt in their pieces. The resulting diversity is a reflection of the diversity of academic fields, genres and personal expressions represented by the authors.[1]

Mary Daly wrote long ago that, "Women have had the power of naming stolen from us."[2] The quest for our own naming, and our own language, is never-ending, and each of us attempts it differently.

The editors wish to note that The Morrigan is known by a variety of titles and spellings—and is associated with many other Goddesses. We chose not to police how contributors addressed Her.

People often get caught up on whether we say *Goddess* or *Girl God* or *Divine Female* vs. *Divine Feminine*. Personally, I try to just listen to what the speaker is trying to say. The fact remains that few of us were privileged with a woman-affirming education—and

---

1   This paragraph is borrowed and adapted with love from *A Jihad for Justice: Honoring the Work and Life of Amina Wadud*. Edited by Kecia Ali, Juliane Hammer and Laury Silvers.
2   Daly, Mary. *Gyn/Ecology: The Metaethics of Radical Feminism*. Beacon Press, 1990.

we all have a lot of time to make up for. Let's all be gentle with each other through that process.

If you find that a particular writing doesn't sit well with you, please feel free to use the Al-Anon suggestion: "Take what you like, leave the rest!" That said, if there aren't at least several pieces that challenge you, we have not done our job here.

I also want to address the fact that some people who follow Girl God Books seemed to take issue with publishing an anthology about a Warrior Goddess. I really liked what Stephanie Woodfield wrote about the word:

> "Warrior is a term that means many things to different people and may not be appropriate for you. That's perfectly okay. The Morrigan gives us each different marching orders, if you will. Being a devotee of the Morrigan means you are cultivating a deep connection with this particular Irish goddess; it doesn't mean you've been spiritually recruited into the Morrigan's army."[3]

Although I am against war, I am a firm believer in self-defense—and the protection of women children above all else. I was once described by a reader as a "Peaceful Warrior digging New Ground."

Personally, I think anyone who is afraid of the word *warrior* should take a closer look at themselves, their own (relative) privilege and the realities of most women around the world. Learn about the Gulabi Gang in India and tell me we don't desperately need women warriors. As Malcolm X said, "Concerning non-violence: it is criminal to teach people not to defend themselves when they are the victims of constant brutal attacks."

---

3   Woodfield, Stephanie. *Priestess of The Morrigan: Prayers, Rituals, & Devotional Work to the Great Queen*. Llewellyn Publications; 2021.

Whatever your thoughts, there are a variety of viewpoints expressed in this anthology—and you are sure to learn something from each of them.

For me, I am comfortable with my middle-aged Mama Bear Warrior Queen persona. As Sonia Johnson wrote: "I am a warrior in the time of women warriors; the longing for justice is the sword I carry."

Each anthology that we put out has had a particular flavor. This book was at times a bit out of my comfort zone—but that is exactly the best place to be. May The Morrigan continue to stretch us all to be our best selves and create lives worthy of Warrior Queens.

Casting the Circle of The Great Queen

Nikki Wardwell Sleath

Among other things, I am a witch, healer, founder and leader of a large, private magickal order and long-term devotee of The Morrigan. As the Great Queen has been entwined in my heart and my magickal practice in a profound way for so many years and has shown herself in her many guises to represent a balanced force of the classical magickal elements, I wanted to share these words of calling her in all of her elemental forms to grace the quarters of the sacred circle. I hope these words help you to connect to the wholeness of her magick, and to enhance and hallow your own sacred space.

"I call to you, Nemhain, and your elements of the East, and of Air. Raven shifter, whipping frenzied tempests... Bringer of tests and riddles that challenge the mind and warp perceptions... Feathered winds of sword-sharp inspiration, I am honored by your presence in this circle.

I call to you, Macha, and your elements of the South, and of Fire. Red-haired queen, stallion-racing champion of stalwart persistence and courage... Rainer of flame, Wolf-sprinting, spearpoint dancer and lady of passion, fueling the ability to influence and win battles, I am honored by your presence in this circle.

I call to you, Babd, and your elements of the West, and of Water. Knowing prophetess, seer, bringer of magickal verses... Riverside washer of the vestments flowing between life and death, Eel-curving, electrifying and conducting, allowing vision into the cauldron of mysteries, I am honored by your presence in this circle.

I call to you, Anu, and your elements of the North, and of Earth. Embedded in the land, bestowing sovereignty and responsibility... Queen of the Mounds of the Otherworld and of the sacred speaking stone... Woman of the heifer's power and the ultimate ability to rule, I am honored by your presence in this circle.

I call to you, An Morrioghain, and your elements of the Center, of Spirit. Spark of mystery uniting heart and soul, embodiment of deep spiritual mystery and the nature of life and death... Giver and taker, bringer of truths that cut through the questions of mortality and self and ring the resounding call to a higher purpose. I accept your challenge and am honored by your presence in this circle. Go raibh maith agat."

The Great Queen

Andrea Redmond

Painted In Blood & Woad

Phoenix Angelis

Lines painted in Woad upon her face.
Blood etched like Tears beneath her eyes.
The tears an Ocean.
Of Pain, Of Grief.
Of Battles Lost & Won.
The war still to be fought.
She looks up at the brush of Raven Wings.
Enfolded in their dark warmth.
Her gaze upon Her face.
Called there by Her touch.
As She paints the Crescent upon her brow.
Claiming Her Daughter.
Naming her Priestess.
Life & Death entwined in beauty on Her face.
Half calling forth a Mother in her Fullness.
The other the stark white Bone of Decay.

The Raven Queen.
Banshee Call of the Battlefield.
Mistress of Land & Sovereignty.
Ever changing Shapeshifter.
Washer At The Ford
Culler & Caller of The Mighty Dead.
Morrigan, The Phantom Queen.
Dark Mother
Though she knows not wholly why She has Chosen her.
She rises Painted in Blood & Woad.
Answering The Morrigan's call.
The Call of The Great Queen.

Call of The Morrigan

Jessica Johnson

The first time I can remember the Morrigan entering my consciousness was on a birthday hike up a grueling mountain in my city. My birthday is in the summer, and I didn't want to encounter many people on my hike. So, to increase the meditative experience, I left the house around 6:30 AM, drove to the base, and began my ascent. The hike starts off rather easily, a few stairs to get you deeper into the woods, and then a decently steep, but not outrageous, well-cut path zig-zagging up the side. You climb pretty quickly, but not at an exhausting rate. Soon though, the path narrows considerably and the real climbing begins. There are steps set into the side at various points, and there are even a couple of makeshift benches built along the side, just simple boards nailed between two trees.

Then, suddenly, you stop climbing for a time, and you walk along a relatively flat, well-shaded area where a lot of flowering, ground covering plants are mixed in with the ferns. You can see the sky through the canopy, and no matter whether there's wind or not, it's a place you can often hear the trees whispering to each other. It was at this spot that I felt moved to reach out to the Morrigan for the first time.

As I walked into the grove, three crows began to talk to each other, all right over my head, surrounding me on both of my sides, and one before me. They couldn't have been more than 20 feet over my head, and the one in front of me kept *looking* at me, pointedly. Without even knowing what I was doing, or saying, I said out loud "Oh Morrigan, may I please have leave to enter your sacred wood?" These must have been the magick words, because at that moment all three crows lifted off their branches, and making a great deal of noise flew off in the direction of the path before me. I took that as a yes, and I followed.

Now, what I had thought had felt like sacred ground gave way to a quiet, little used fork of the path, and I chose to go down it. I turned a corner of the path and I was suddenly in this quiet, peaceful little area. I knew I had come to where the crows had wanted me to be, because literally, right at my feet, was a beautiful, perfect, freshly fallen crow's feather. I picked it up, and removed my pack. I sat down on the edge of the path and I closed my eyes as I leaned my back against a giant cedar tree. I don't know how long I stayed there like that. I don't even remember if I really "made contact" with the Morrigan in my meditation, but I remember the feeling of being home that I experienced there, and the calm that had come over me. I'll never forget that moment.

Nothing much came of that day in the woods for quite some time. I did a bit of research on the Morrigan when I got home, and I did start to see more crow feathers on my walks and in my backyard, but life got very busy for me shortly after that, and much of what I knew about the Morrigan got tucked into the back of my mind.

Fast forward four years later; I was in my sacred circle in front of my altar on the night of Imbolc, lit only by candles and breathing in the heavy scent of Nag Champa incense and narcissus blossoms. I had heard quite a bit more about the Morrigan over the last four years, and felt a twinge of jealousy that she has chosen other people, but not me. Still feeling like I was on the quest for a deity to *really* connect with, I picked up an oracle deck, shuffled, and pulled a card.

The Morrigan.

I was dumbstruck. There are only a few actual goddesses or deities in this deck. The rest are fae figures from legends and myths. I could feel my heart pounding a little bit. I decided to meditate on this card, and as I did, I gradually came to understand that she felt I had been avoiding her long enough. I felt a little confused, wondering if I had manifested this card with my longing, or if this was a genuine experience. The next morning, I made a cup of tea, and pulled out the same deck. I rifle shuffled. I hand-over-hand shuffled. I cut the deck and moved it around and shuffled some more. I pulled another card, searching for clarity regarding the previous night's reading.

The Morrigan.

It was then that I felt a bit scared. I knew a little bit about the Morrigan, but I also knew a lot of people talked about her being a very fierce and even dangerous goddess. Have I awoken her wrath? I pulled up my laptop and opened a browser and brought up YouTube. And I kid you not, on the home page were a bunch of video recommendations. They were all videos about the Morrigan. I took my first, tentative sip of tea, took a deep breath like I was preparing to dive, and I clicked on the first video. I knew it was time to stop running.

Over the next few days, I became familiar with some people on YouTube that I had already known a little bit about, but now also know that they are followers of the Morrigan too. Some of them talk about the darker aspects of the Morrigan, some about the lighter, but all have nothing but respect and admiration for their matron goddess. The darkness they talk about is also intriguing. They are referencing shadow work, facing fears, and shedding masks or skins they have worn for protection over the years that the Morrigan has helped them with. These people—all of them—have been transformed by the work they've done with their goddess. They are in awe of her, reverent of her, and not one of them regrets the work they've done, even if the journey has been a difficult one.

My tea had long gone cold, which for me, first thing in the morning, is pretty much unheard of. I shut the lid of my laptop and took the tea to the kitchen, nuked it in the microwave (I can't stand cold tea...) and went to go look out my office window, into my backyard. Hot tea yet again in hand, I stood there at the window, sipping slowly. Somehow, I had lucked out that my husband and kids were all still in bed, and I'd been given this time of peace and quiet to reflect, to think. I was staring blankly off into space at the bare, damp soil of my garden when suddenly, a Stellar's Jay flew onto the very spot I was staring at. That roused my attention!

Stellar's Jays are my favorite bird, ever. And that's saying something because I am a bird nerd in general. They're sometimes called the Western Blue Jay, and are crested like a Blue Jay, but are all black on the top half of their bodies, and then it blends into a beautiful shiny deep blue on their bottom half. They have a loud squawk and are a member of the crow family. Some people find them quite annoying, but I personally love their spunky personality, quick wit, intelligence, and their striking beauty. What really roused me from my ponderings though, was the fact that one was in my yard. You see, we had moved into this townhouse about a year before, and there weren't a lot of trees in our area. Jays need the trees for nesting, and so while I heard them in the trees of the more settled area around our complex, they rarely flew where I could see them. I had tried everything to entice them to my balcony, including peanuts, suet, but all I managed to attract were a couple of black squirrels.

This jay flew down to the spot of soil I had been gazing blankly at, and hopped around, looking for something to eat. It pecked at the ground a few times, and obviously finding nothing of interest, flew onto my balcony rail which was level the window I was standing at. It turned its back to my house, giving me the perfect profile look at her (I instinctively dubbed it a her, though in truth it could have been either gender), and then squawked as loud as it could a few times. I could hear the echo of other jays in the distance, and then, with just a quick glance at me, it took off in the direction of the calls.

I stood there, stunned, for a few moments, and then, the message hit me, like a shockwave. The voice in my head, though whispered, was clear as a bell, and carried a force behind it.

"Join us, Daughter."

Well. That was about all it took for me to heed the Call of the Morrigan. I have proudly called myself her daughter ever since. Over the years since these events, I have been through a lot, but constantly felt the strength and guidance of The Morrigan. Her presence has comforted me when nothing else could, and she has helped me to face my demons in a way I think no other goddess could. Most of all, she's awoken the warrior in me, encouraging me to fight for what is right for myself and my family, and in the world around me. She's helped me come out of my shell, and show the world who I truly am.

Throughout this book you will read more stories from people who have come to heed the call of The Morrigan through different, but equally powerful and meaningful experiences. Working with this ancient, little understood goddess in the modern day is no easy feat, but if it is one thing that's become clear to a lot of us, it is that she's back with a vengeance! We will explore many facets of The Morrigan in this book, but especially her warrior queen aspect. The consensus a lot of the time seems to be that she calls her sons and daughters to her side to help her fight for justice, and for righting wrongs, and implores the wounded healers to stand up and fight, and share their vulnerability, to create powerful change and transformation within their personal lives and communities. If you too have heard the Morrigan's call, this book will help you open up to the reserves of strength, power, endurance, compassion and healing that reside within all of us. If The Morrigan is new to you, then I hope that you will walk away from this journey with a deeper understanding and appreciation for the sons and daughters that have answered this call, and chosen to walk along an often more difficult path, in order to bring about the justice of The Morrigan.

The Morrigan
Lisbeth Cheever-Gessaman

When the Warrior Doesn't Win

Barbara Whiterose Marie McSweeney PhD

"Shame upon you all for showing no respect or pity for me at this time! You will pay a heavy price for your cruelty."[4]

Macha, the Goddess in human form, condemns the crowd of bystanders. Unmoved, they watch mercilessly as she, heavily pregnant, runs a race, exerting herself nearly to the point of death. She wins, delivers twins, and collapses. Afterward, all the men in the crowd fall down too.

Macha addresses them again: "From this day on you will be afflicted by this weakness because of your cruel treatment of me. At the hour of your greatest need, when you are under attack, every Ulsterman will become as defenceless and helpless as a woman giving birth to a child. For five days and four nights you will remain in that state and your descendants will be afflicted by the same weakness for nine generations!"[5]

The first time I heard Macha's admonishment and curse, rendered above in Mary Heaney's words, I received a sudden and indelible vision of the Goddess: upright and powerful, staring fiercely at us all and indicting us for our inaction.

"Us," you ask? Yes, us. I pictured her on stage, striding toward the edge of the proscenium to address the crowd in the theater, as we too sat silent and passive, watching the show.

---

4 Marie Heaney, "The Weakness of the Ulstermen," in Heaney, *Over Nine Waves: A Book of Irish Legends* (London/Boston: Faber and Faber, 1994), 67. I first heard the story when Tom Cowan read it aloud in his workshop, Celtic Shamanism and the Druid Wisdom Tales, at the University of St, Mary's of the Lake in Mundelein, Illinois in August 2008.

5 Heaney, "The Weakness of the Ulstermen," 68.

This image of Macha's furious confrontation was the initial inspiration for my opera, *Weakness,* a retelling of "The Weakness of the Ulstermen." The Ulstermen's incapacity—their inability to protect themselves from violence—is the direct consequence of their refusal to protect Macha from a fatal ordeal. The warrior Goddess renders the human warriors impotent. This is the "heavy price" they pay for their inhumanity.

My *Weakness,* though, refers not so much to the curse she places on the craven bystanders *after* the fatal race, but rather to the human weaknesses that allow the race even to take place. Individual flaws and societal failings lead to three betrayals. The first is from Macha's mortal husband, who, despite promising to keep her identity a secret, boasts about her physical prowess, exclaiming, "My wife can run faster than the King's horses!" The King, his pride wounded, his resentment kindled, demands that Macha race against his horses. Macha implores him:

> *I can win, but the price will be too high.*
> *Will you not spare me?*

The second betrayal: He refuses to pardon her and threatens to kill her husband.

Macha turns to the crowd:

> *Will no one help me? No one?*
> *Is there not one among you whose blood flows warm within?*
> *No one?*
> *Have I no sister? No brother? No one?*[6]

---

6   This and all remaining citations of the Macha story are from Barbara White, *Weakness* (2012) or from oral tradition. Sound recording on Albany/Troy 1441 (2013). The recording also includes Tom Cowan's *Macha.* Also see Frank J. Oteri, "Barbara White: A Plea for Compassion," *NewMusicBox,* March 1, 2018.

No reply. This is the third betrayal, made in silence. The King's subjects stand still and stony-faced. They turn their backs, afraid to confront the King, or ashamed to be seen by the Goddess, or perhaps merely apathetic.

Sacrificed in turn by a prideful husband, an envious King, and a passive-aggressive citizenry, Macha challenges them all, in righteous indignation:

> *Who among you dares to stand with me?*
> *Who among you will not hide in silence?*
> *Who among you has never fallen and cried out?*
> *Who among you has not been broken?*
> *Who among you hasn't known the kindness of a mother?*
> *Who among you is not a part of me?*

But still there is no response, no empathy. "Let her show us what she can do," the monarch taunts, determined to do her in. As she predicted, she wins, and as she also predicted, the price has been too high. She is victorious and defeated at the same time.

Is the Goddess in human form betrayed, too, by us? We spectators form a crowd, the one that sits in the comfortable seats in the theater, drinking in the myth acted out in front of us. Why do we assemble to watch the Goddess suffer? Is this a cautionary tale or an instruction manual? When we leave the theater, what roles do we play?

As in the story of Macha, everyday life is replete with wrongdoing. A man-boy appropriates a woman's words as his own; a scholar sabotages a peer's reputation out of spite; a witness fails to act because they fear being appointed the next scapegoat. A woman is resented, shunned, and erased, all in retaliation for her gifts, wisdom, and expertise. These are just a few that I have experienced. Others have other stories, surely. The human failings depicted in the Macha story are ever present among us mortals.

I worry about the modern-day myth I encounter so often: the one that assures girls and women that if we are just self-knowledgeable enough, determined enough, and confident enough, we will flourish and thrive. Women have always had self-knowledge, determination, and confidence, but we haven't always flourished or thrived. Boldness and defiance are not always welcomed.

Some things are stronger than us. We can be overrun by unwarranted power, by male supremacy, by a zero-sum mentality, and by our families' passive negligence or active disregard. In a woman-hating culture, spunk is not enough. Nor is a warrior spirit; some warriors lose.

And this is where Sovereignty comes in. Tom Cowan points out that we may not always be in control, but even when we are not in control we can be in charge. Macha, having assumed human form, is susceptible to human suffering and vulnerable to injury and death, but she remains in charge. After the King threatens her husband's life, she agrees to run the race, but she does not accept or condone the King's show of force. She does not bow to him. She does not apologize or cower or appease. Instead, she roars her uncompromising truth to patriarchal power. She stands in righteousness and condemns the weak ones who have sent her to the slaughter.

Still, assuming the moral high ground does not guarantee success in the face of wrongdoing. I learned this from Macha, the hard way. Naively, I expected others to value Macha and her lessons about Sovereignty. This turned out to be true in large part, but even so, the production of *Weakness* was tarnished by professional, personal, and institutional betrayal. The story of Macha refused to confine itself to the stage, seeping out to contaminate the work of presenting it. Life imitated art.

An elder pointed out to me, "One person cannot change a culture," but I thought I could. I insisted that I could. I knew what had gone wrong. I thought the aggressors just needed to be instructed and enlightened—that their sense of decency, or at least their capacity for shame, would lead them to seek remedy in collaboration and community. But the inverse turned out to be true: They showed no sense of decency or capacity for shame.

Eight years later, the retaliation against my transgression—that is, my refusal to be subservient, to give my work away, to appease a mob—has not let up even a bit. This is painful to disclose, for tucked inside every story of victimization is the knowledge that revealing the story puts one at risk of even more degradation.

I have journeyed with Macha for twelve years now, and she remains elusive. Her gifts come in the form not of attainment but of awareness. Macha reminds me that, no matter how much self-knowledge, determination, and confidence I have, and no matter how right I may be, I am not omnipotent. Boldness and defiance don't cut it with those who thirst for domination. On the contrary, a woman's forthrightness, power, and self-respect may be what triggers aggressors to attack. As in the story of Macha, a woman's strength may bring out others' weaknesses.

Sometimes a woman tries to negotiate a patriarchal bargain, thinking that if she accommodates and appeases, and if she sells out other women, she will gain respect and camaraderie from the club. But in doing so, she sacrifices Sovereignty, and she will never, ever receive genuine respect from those to whom she has ceded her integrity and personal power. She will be reminded constantly that her success is an illusion, a pretense offered only at the pleasure of the King. And the King, knowing she knows this, need do nothing more to remind her she is not really a member of the club. She already knows. I've seen at least one woman ruined by her efforts to grovel, to placate, and to serve as proxy for male-pattern aggression. I've also seen men shunned when they refuse

24

to join in the dance of domination: When a man declines to betray women, thereby forgoing solidarity with men, he too risks being snubbed and smeared.

When I see women caught between the Scylla of compliance and the Charybdis of resistance, Macha reminds me that many, many women and men in human history have lived without full control over their destinies—most people, I would think—but have nevertheless found ways to be in charge. Honoring one's own integrity and personal power in the face of disenfranchisement is one way to embrace Sovereignty—even when one must stand alone.[7]

After the race and the birth of her twins, Macha finds herself depleted, at the end of her human life. In most portrayals, she exacts revenge, ferociously cursing the crowd so that they will be thwarted by weakness when confronted in battle. However, my Macha does not level a curse at those who betrayed her. She knows, in her wisdom, that it's not necessary:

> *When the people suffer, it is this story that they tell.*
> *They say that I cursed them, but no, they cursed themselves.*
> *When they most needed their strength, it would fail them.*
> *When they hungered for the harvest, their earth would give them nothing.*
> *When they were thirsty, the well would run dry.*
> *And when they most needed another, no one would come.*
> *That was their doing, not mine.*

---

7   Jessica Johnson depicts the Goddess's integrity: "As Macha, I am a protector goddess, and you can call on me when you are scared. I will help you to not be afraid, and to stand up for what is right." (Jessica Johnson, *My Name is The Morrigan* [The Girl God Books, 2018, Kindle Edition], 28.) Tom Cowan's *Macha* (n. 3) ends with an acknowledgment of Macha's isolation: "But whatever happened to her, Macha is still present whenever people fall in love, make promises, or need courage to stand alone against the crowd."

The prideful husband, vindictive King, and spineless bystanders have created their own prison. Their betrayals led to their downfall—not because they were punished by a Goddess, but because they betrayed themselves. By failing to stand against domination, they ceded their own power and destroyed any remnant of compassion for one another. No retaliation was necessary. Macha the warrior knew the battle had ended and the aggressors had been vanquished.

It's hard to stop here. Tropes of triumph and redemption call out, tempting me to find some way to say Macha has prevailed—and that, by extension, I, and all women, might too. But that would be denying that personal power can be ineffectual in the face of domination and woman-hating. The warrior doesn't always win.

But she does hold firm. We may be denied control, but we can still be in charge. In the end, sometimes all we have is Sovereignty, and sometimes that has to be enough.

Macha's Curse

Stephanie Woodfield

They thought they were greater than you.
Stronger than you,
more powerful than you,
more important than you.
Unquestioned in their cruelty,
and you a woman,
pregnant, unprotected.
No threat to the men of Ulster.
Yet still you pleaded with them.
Have mercy,
did not a mother bare you?
Have mercy,
looks can deceive.
I have power,
I have strength,
I have speed,
I know the words of power,
to bless,
to heal,
to curse,
to cripple,
to bring justice,
to bring low the men of Ulster.
If you will not hear me with the woman's voice,
I will curse you with a crow's voice.

Crow Woman: Morrigan of Sacred Wrath

Iriome R. Martín Alonso

Morrigan, Mother of Sacred Wrath: Why Being Angry is Necessary

Iriome R. Martín Alonso

When I was nineteen I moved to Maynooth (Maigh Nuadhad, "plain of Nuadha") in county Kildare for a year. I was doing my Erasmus[8] and was also very sick. Though I don't like remembering things about that time often, it was the place where I learnt that even if we can contact deities and spirits all over the world no matter where we are, nothing compares to actually visiting the place where they were born, the place and culture they are.

I felt the heartbeats of The Morrigan pulsating under a land that covers Her in concrete, claiming to worship a foreign god but remembering Her; never going around hollow hills at night, never cutting ribbon-filled trees even if they interfere with traffic because "they are from the Sídhe"; and leaving offerings at crossroads of milk and honey and never coming back for them on solstice nights.

Crows stole food from my neighbours who were mad as banshees with them. Some (not the majority) even tried to poison them. I saw this and vowed to Morrigan that I'd feed them as long as I was in Éire. It was the first thing I ever did each morning: I went out, called Her and fed Her crows, rooks, magpies and ravens. First three, then ten, once around thirty. They knew me, followed me. They brought black cats to eat at my house too and I also fed them.

I felt Her sovereignty in the circles of Emain Macha, in the needles that made my fingers swallow, at the Lia Fáil stone at Tara, the

---

8 European Community Action Scheme for the Mobility of University Students. It's a Higher Education exchange programme for students, teachers and institutions, run in the UK by the British Council.

depths of the passage tombs of NewGrange, sharing space with Sheela Na-Gig in Clonmacnoise, singing at the Cliffs of Moher, in the darkness of the Doolin cave and rising in the tongues of those who speak the land's language in Connemara.

I'm not afraid of Morrigan, but I respect Her as the Ancient Queen She is. She has been fierce and towering, but I've never been frightened in Her presence; on the contrary, She has granted me self-power and confidence. I'm not a person that fears their gods, I admire them and create a bond of reverence; in my former experience in another religion, fearing deities was toxic and counterproductive. A father/mother/whatever figure should be loved and honored, but never feared. Huge red flags there, my dears.

The Morrigan was a popular goddess in ancient times, and she's become very popular in contemporary paganism. We have plenty, though christianised, versions of Her myths in folklore, manuscripts, art and song. Some writers such as the Matthews[9] would even say She remained through the Arthurian legends under the guise or Morgan le Fey; some others[10] will claim that despite their evident closeness and similar attributes they are different deities with Morgana coming from Welsh "Mori Gena" meaning "born from the Sea" or "Modron," "the Mother" and Morrigan from Irish "Great/Phantom Queen." Whatever the truth is, as Demelza Fox[11] says, there's no denying that they share plenty in common – such as the crow as their main animal, their shape-shifting nature, their Sovereign demeanour and the fairy and fate link. In addition, their stories with heroes are often similar – how

---

9   Matthews, C. (25 January 1992). *Ladies of the Lake*. Thorsons. & Matthews, John (25 March 2003). *Sir Gawain: Knight of the Goddess*. Inner Traditions / Bear & Co.
10 Clark, Rosalind (1990). *The Great Queens: Irish Goddesses from the Morrígan to Cathleen Ní Houlihan*. Irish Literary Studies. Book 34.
11 Fox, D. (20 July 2020). *Morgan le Fay Summer School* [Online Course]. Rockstar Priestess. https://rockstarpriestess.teachable.com/p/morgan-le-fay-summer-school

they granted their downfall through the use of their sexuality when they wronged Them and weren't true to their words.

In a lot of Goddess-based spiritualities they/we tend to eliminate Goddesses of War considering them "allies to the patriarchy" (i.e., Athena, Inanna, Trebaruna, Morrigan Herself), based in books with little to no archaeological evidence as well as no regard for history. I do agree that re-writing herstory is necessary, imperative even, but not on the foundations of idealistic lies that do us no good; what's most important is that we are mutilating a part of ourselves in the process when we claim Goddesses of War should be extinguished or are a corruption, depraved version of all-nurturing mothering ones. The truth is, they are normally both.

An ideal world where Goddess values are revered is something we should be inspired by and work together into manifesting on Earth, but based on real knowledge, evidence, fact. What is the difference, then, between those who claim to work with the shadow and at the same time renegade from wrath – and New Age rhetoric (or even male monotheistic faiths) that repress our darkness to pursue a fabricated ideal of "purity" that is simply not real? If we choose arbitrarily what shadows can be included in our personal and collective narrative, are we being honest with ourselves or just choosing what makes us less uncomfortable?

Violence is natural to all creatures and to Nature Herself. Have you ever witnessed a birth? That's the first act of violence we endure, when we are taken away from the soft, warm embrace of the womb that shelters us, feeds us and protects us into a dry, stimulus-filled world that blinds us just as we open our eyes before we can ever hear our parent's heartbeats. But being born is necessary to live, no matter how violent it is.

Now, I'm not making an apology for violence – or going about traumatising people and feeling grateful for our trauma. You shouldn't. That bullshit of "We made a pact before we were born

31

to experience blah blah blah" must end. It makes the victim of horrible experiences guilty and it's not fair or healthy. We may comfort ourselves temporarily with a discourse of "everything happens for a reason." but these words are cold comfort. This is not always the truth. Yes, sometimes things do happen for a reason, but sometimes that reason is that people are just mean, selfish, or evil. Goddess doesn't want you to suffer. Morrigan specifically would aid you and give you strength in moments of need, sometimes through anger. We humans tend to be imbalanced and go to limits that shouldn't be crossed, and the violence that exists in the world now is nothing but horrible and terrifying. My point is that denying the rage in ourselves also devours us from the inside and deprives us from amazing, life-saving tools.

Morrigan teaches us that wrath protects us. We feel angry and upset when our limits are being crossed, when we feel in danger, when injustice happens before us. And, you know what? That's wonderful! Anger, unlike sadness, makes us act. It makes us super alive. And what's in a Goddess-based spirituality without real, material action? We put ourselves in a safe place, we run for shelter, we stand firm against non-physical attacks, we don't let people be hurt in our presence.

My therapist told me last year that being angry and alert was what actually saved me from being raped, because it made me act quickly with a cold mind. That way of violence toward women has to be ended forever and also must be severely punished – but acting in cold rage kept me safe.

In a way, allowing ourselves to feel anger is also letting Goddess' Justice flow through us. "Yeah, but who am I to judge? Only gods can judge." You're a person. Goddess lives in you, you're Her, She's you too. I'm not telling you to go out at night throwing punches but maybe you don't have to be a pagan nun either.

What's a "pagan nun?"

I guess you've heard the so-called "light workers," again, denying darkness saying, "We gotta send light and compassion even to rapists/murderers/pedophiles/whatever horrible criminal." Maybe you yourself agree with that, under the premise that they are "sick" people that "need forgiveness the most."

It is those who were traumatized by these "sick" people who most need our compassion—a child who must endure abuse and develops a neurodivergent brain to keep being alive; a suicidal woman who was raped; a person raised in a neglectful family that is depressed; any type of human with mental health issues. In this case, perhaps someone who isn't fully able to carry the life they want for themselves, but at least is living a life with some balance and peace.

Now, the pagan nun (or monk) is what I like to call pagan devotees or priest/esses that not only deny anger, but carry some particularly christian mindset, substituting mercy or pity with "compassion."

The last couple of years, I've been made to feel like I'm not a compassionate person because I refuse to turn the other cheek and do nothing about severe injustices that occurred with no other consequences from those in charge but a scolding – and a feigned "regret" by the perpetrator without making amends. Sound familiar? It looks a lot like the catholic rite of confession.

The paradigm of the pagan nun, all-forgiving, never bothered, never angry, never acting, is just a consequence of conversion. Now, based on what I've experienced, studied and seen, many pagans are converts, meaning we weren't raised pagan and a huge percentage of us come from other religions rather than from an atheist or agnostic background. This makes some belief transfers inevitable – such as how priestesses should behave, ethics, morals and ways of faith – in how we mix old stories, ancient Goddesses and our former cosmovision. This makes a huge mess, because we are pushed to do shadow, healing and Underworld work while at the same time feeling ashamed by our communities and ourselves for going through non-accepted processes. Sadness? Trauma? Pain? All good, buddy, but being angry? Standing up for yourself? Saying "No?" Questioning things? That means you're troubled, problematic, and they don't want that.

The Morrigan is a Warrior Queen that embodies the Sovereignty of the Land,[12] an archetype often forgotten that showcases the figure of Queen not as one who has "power over," but rather "power within" – from ancestral times in Éire, the rite of the *Marriage of the Land*[13] consisted of the ruler, mostly the king, having to "marry" the land and being substituted or even sacrificed if it didn't prosper.

Of course, we can't be going in our lives just discarding people or ending relationships with them because they do something wrong. We must be understanding, empathetic and give second chances – but it has lit a spark in me thinking about the ongoing theme of unhealthy forgiveness. Why should we forgive people "just because" when they keep hurtful habits with no desire or intent to work on them, sometimes even for years or decades? Forgiveness is key for our healing, but we don't have to let people's dynamics, abuse and disrespect into our circles. Morrigan

12 Green, Miranda. *Celtic Goddesses: Warriors, Virgins, and Mothers*; (1995) British Museum Press, London & Bhreathnach, Máire. 1982. "The Sovereignty Goddess as Goddess of Death?" Zeitschrift für celtische Philologie.

13 National Museum or Ireland - Archaeology. (n.d.). *Kingship and Sacrifice | Archaeology*. Retrieved 2016, from https://www.museum.ie/en-IE/Museums/Archaeology/Exhibitions/Kingship-and-Sacrifice Herbert, Máire. 1992. "Goddess and King: The Sacred Marriage in Early ireland." In *Women and Sovereignty*, edited by Louise Olga Fradenburg, 264–75. Edinburgh: University of Edinburgh Press.

strips "hero" Cú Chulainn[14] from his luck in battle, which She had favoured, when he denied Her and defied Her, and we can take this episode not as a matter of divine pride but of self-respect, because even if people or society has made you not love yourself enough, you should always respect yourself first and foremost, and stepping away from what or who hurts you is not cowardice, but a gesture of great courage, no matter how hard it is.

Should I forgive the people of my former Goddess community that made me homeless while I was severely sick just because I didn't support the racism, trans exclusion, lies, sick dynamics, lack of transparency and abuse in rituals? No. And no matter who tells you what, following one's principles and being angry doesn't make you evil or a monster. It means you understand what loyalty is even if you have no one else to be loyal to – because you remain true to yourself, and you should never have to forgive yourself for that.

Morrigan is from the Sídhe[15] too, and Warrior-faery Goddesses remind us of our instinct, of what keeps us not just surviving but also fully living. What aligns with your true nature? There's no shame in being proud of who we are, and the fire of Morrigan's spirit will fuel us when we shine the dimmest. Maybe we don't wanna be a distant and cold star if we'd been cast away from a constellation, but we can be transformed into a blazing forest fire made flesh.

Morrigan is also a witch who tells us that curses are a tool She's taught us to keep us safe. If I had told five-year-old Iriome (who was then a "good witch," making protective and health spells) that old her would cast curses and hex rapists on the nights of Dark

---

14 Táin Bó Regamna & Táin Bó Cúalnge from the *Book of Leinster* (in Irish and English), CELT : The Corpus of Electronic Texts. & Ulster Cycle.

15 Rankine, D., D'Este, S., & Andrews, B. (2019). *The Guises of the Morrigan: The Celtic Irish Goddess of Battle & Sovereignty: Her Myths, Powers and Mysteries* (2nd ed.). Avalonia.

Moon, she wouldn't have believed it – but I know she would understand it if I could explain to her now. Some people might be anti-cursing and that's okay, or believe in the threefold law or "karma," but I say, why wait for karma if you can be karma yourself? We are the embodiment of Goddess, if we don't act, who will? As the story of Rhiannon tells us, we have to ask the Goddess or She cannot provide.

Pagan witches use Her power to change reality, not only with spells but also with actions that shape what's around us. Do you believe a spell is just kindling some candles with a deep enigmatic voice? Calling out someone to stop crossing your limits is way more effective and less wax consuming.

What Goddesses of War evidence is that we live in a dichotomic society that has separated things that have always been whole, trying to strip us from the very tools that would protect us from the horrors it created, and also vulnerating a part of us so badly that those concepts have transgressed religions and conversions of faith until embedded in every last bit of our collective memory. We feel guilty for saying "No" – the best banishing spell we can cast. What Morrigan reminds us, from all of Europe to the ancient land of Éire, is that wrath is a sign that we are alive, that we care for ourselves and others, that these are things that matter even if we haven't experienced them or belong to the communities that suffer. She will be there listening intently to our troubles, raising us from the floor when we're having a crisis alone... in the sound of the ravens warning you from storms and taking you out of the forest when you're lost... in every sister that will defend you... in every safe boundary, every act of deconstruction... and in the flame that boils in you when Her anger fuels you to keep you safe.

Let Her fierce love come through.

Woman of Fire and Solar Alchemy:
My Personal Vision of The Morrighan

Arlene Bailey

A few months ago, I began having dreams of The Morrighan, but not like anything I ever learned or knew about her. In my dreams and visions, my journeys, she came to me as a Woman of Fire... A Goddess of burning shift and desire with a light so bright one could not look directly upon her. Though I knew her as a Shapeshifter, the vision she showed me was not the dark winged one, but rather that of the alchemist at her forge pounding darkness until it shapeshifted into brilliant light. Though not her primary interpretation according to the lore, this was my personal gnosis and I knew the truth of the visions she wrapped me in, heard the messages she brought and they were her visage as a Solar Alchemist, a Goddess of the Sun shining and burning with the fire of truth and sovereignty that lights our fire within.

She left me with the following...

Out of the darkness of history,
I rise as the brightly shining sun.

Shapeshifting into a Goddess of
burning transformation and desire,
with a fire so bright one dare
not look directly upon me.

I am The Morrighan... Warrioress,
Queen, Shapeshifter, She of Prophecy,
Keeper of the Forge and more, but
now I come to you as a Woman of Fire,
Goddess of the Sun, Solar Alchemist.

As the caw of the black winged one
carries me in both darkness and light,
I am the visage of the many
and the Alchemy of the All.

Arlene Bailey, ©2021

Magic and Mystery: Answering Her Call

Arlene Bailey

The Morrighan Speaks

Arlene Bailey

You fear me, don't you?
Your heart filled with
dread at the very sight
of my blood soaked face,
the sword in my hand

But we are not so different
You and I, and though you
think I called you, it was
you who called to me

For I am She who will take
your dross, molding and shaping
and forging it in the fire
until you stand in your gold
speaking your truth

I am She who will continue
to challenge you as you
grow and shift into the mighty
warrioress you are meant to be
The black raven soaring above
it all until the day you feel me
in your bones and we are one

You called to me so what
is it you desire? Are you listening?
Daughter of my blood!
Speak!

Though some call Her dark
She lights my way, The Morrighan,
She who takes me to those
deep, dark places of Soul
so that I may fight the battles
that trap and deny me less
than an empowered life

She who paints me with the
bright red of my own blood,
fingers streaking my body with
that sticky, gooey redness that
is my reminder of my mortality
AND my feral desire for life,
but... only on my terms

She who stalks me in my dreams
Calling, calling... cawing, cawing...
Riding in on her nightmare
demanding I pay attention as
Her sword touches my heart
and her blood stained lips
demand verity as She
demands to know...

Have you fought your battles,
Shedding blood to become
who you are?

Are you sufficiently planted in
your deepest knowing such
that you can ride the wind,
knowing your own
wildness, your fierceness?

Can you wield your Sword when
called to, wrestling your prize
away from those who would steal
it and claim it as their own?

Can you face the fires of transformation
as you are forged into a new being?

Will you reign with both mind and heart,
sword and spear, kindness and iron will
speaking with the voice of the poet,
the words of a skilled negotiator, the
rage of one wronged and ignored,
ready to claim what is rightfully yours?

Can you go into battle again and again,
knowing I will pick your bones of all
that is dead, all that no longer serves?

When you can do all these things,
knowing you will be called over and over
to do them again and again, then you
truly wield the sword of a warrioress,
rising as the Phoenix out of the ashes
to claim your embodied sovereignty

As for me, the silky black one of the sky
and the nightmare of your dreams,
the shapeshifter who continues to
challenge and test you, the mother
even who cares and teaches,
molding you with her iron will

Well...

Look for me on the wind and in your
visions, in those unexpected places
and least likely scenarios...

Listen for me for I will always be a part
of you and here to remind you what is
worth going to battle for when you forget
I am here to remind you of your gold
when all you see is death and dross

I am Badb, Macha and Morrigu
Ban Sidhe, Nightmare, Seer,
Conjure Woman, Shape-Shifter
Witch, Warrioress, Queen

I am The Morrighan
and
I have claimed you as mine.

Arlene Bailey, ©2021

Crow Guardian
Arna Baartz

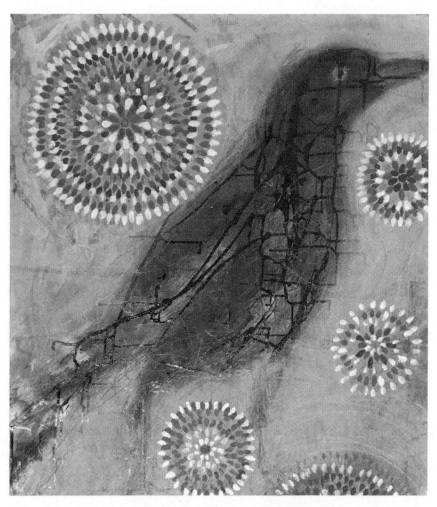

Illustration from *My Name is The Morrigan* by Jessica Johnson

Birth of War

Jaclyn Cherie

My Mother, like Ernmas, gave birth to war.
Born
Sword in one hand
Torch in another,
Inferno
burning inside
Brighter
And
Brighter
Forevermore.
I have fought to exist.
I have fought to live.
Fortified with
Iron,
Steel,
And
An
Insatiable
Desire
To
Resist.
Crows and Corvidae come when I call like
A Legion emerging from thick mist.
You see,
I was born for this.
I have war
Cries
And
Thunders
Rolls
In

My
Soul
Bones.
War is,
I am
A force that can't be
Won't be,
Refuses
To be
Controlled.
War will shake you
To
Your
Core.
You
Aren't
Ready
For
War.
So, please
Leave her alone
Before
She evens the score.

To compare oneself to war is no small statement but it is one that I mean with every fiber of my being:

I am war.

I constantly fight both external and internal battles, and have witnessed so much destruction, violence, loss, and pain that they have become intertwined with my being. All too familiar life companions.

I have been through the war called life.

I have the scars of war.

I have the trauma of war.

I carry the ghosts of war.

Women are supposed to be docile creatures, we are supposed to be delicate and quiet.

I am none of those things.

I am wild as the wolf.

I am solid as the Earth.

And I am loud as the stormiest, raging Seas.

We were not supposed to both make it out alive, my Mom and me.

My birth story, like my life story deserves to be told and it is the start of my war story; *they* always need to be told.

"We are all storytellers in our own right, and those stories deserve to be brought to light."- Jaclyn Cherie

I have always been impatient, but also the most patient person in the world. Ah, the contradictions that have created me.

That impatience is why I decided 3 days after the summer Solstice, nearly 3 months early, on a Sunday that I was going to make my grand entrance into this world.

As dramatic and chaotic as ever.

My Mother was visited by many Goddesses through dreams and other Spiritual messages throughout her pregnancy. She knew what she was facing, not only with how difficult birth would be, but how 'difficult' I would be.

She fought with the strength of 10,000 Women, and somewhere in the Ether, her and I made a pact that neither one of us were going to die that day. Not.That.Day.

I was premature, my lungs were not developed, and my internal systems were not quite strong enough to sustain me just yet.

Doctors warned my Mother after birth how delicate and sensitive I would be; the latter may be correct, as I am emotionally sensitive and a HSP with SPD (Highly Sensitive Person with Sensory Processing Disorder).

Delicate, no.

I had one thing going for me against all those odds: I was angry. I could not breathe without the assistance of oxygen and being inside a box, but I was screaming, shaking with fury, and pissed off.

When my Mom tells the story back, she says that my fury was her sign that I was not only going to survive, but I was going to thrive.

I did not make any step of the Mothering journey easy for her, and even still I give her a run for her money, but when hope has dimmed in my life and I find myself in the quiet recesses of darkness with the void silently screaming my name, I am reminded about that pact we made on a hot summer night in the Ether all that time ago. And, that pact keeps me going for she is my beacon of light and I am the Torchbearer she fought to bear.

"There is only one god, and His name is Death. And there is only one thing we say to Death: 'not today'," Master Syrio Forel, Game of Thrones

When I began doing Ancestral work, and connecting to Deities, energies, and Archetypes that my Ancestors would have, or are known to have had connections to, one of the very first to come through was The Morrigan. It was fitting because Crows, Death and War have been some of the only constants in my life.

I am no stranger to all things dark, scary, and perceived incorrectly, but admittedly She was terrifying.

Like my first encounter with Kali, my first encounter with The Morrigan shook me.

It was the reflection of myself that I saw within them, within Her that scared me the most; the idea that I could somehow also be that terrifying and filled with justified rage.

Or rage in general.

Like I said, there is no quiet and docile over here.

It filled me with a sense of dread and a sense of power. The reconciliation process of those conflicting feelings took years.

As I began to work deeper with my Ancestors and by default The Morrigan, the signs and omens were all around. When She enters your life, when She wants your attention, She is not quiet about it.

Society doesn't like loud Women.

Society doesn't like angry Women.

Society doesn't like Women.

That last statement stings a bit, doesn't it?

Not everyone will agree, but how I see things, how I have experienced them, I know it to be my truth and the truth of many, many Women out there.

Just because society doesn't like something doesn't mean that you, or I shouldn't or can't flaunt it in their face.

I started to become louder.

I started to become angrier.

I started to become unapologetically WOMAN.

I refused to fit into some pre-checked box of what I was supposed to be, how I was supposed to look, and I started living my life how I wanted it to be.

"I flaunt my Femininity and Fluidity in front of the patriarchy and scream like a banshee, for they will see what it means to be me and how it feels to finally break free." -Jaclyn Cherie

Society doesn't like Women, but I refuse to bow down to that pressure.

There are generations of Women, of marginalized people, who came before me and have fought a variation of this fight we face today with their lives so that we could live freer, speak louder and I for one will not let their deaths be in vain.

Women are murdered, kidnapped, and sexually assaulted at staggering numbers.

The world doesn't need docile and quiet, that has gotten us nowhere.

The world needs wild and loud.

The Morrigan has been my personal path to finding my voice because I answered Her call.

Just as your head turns when the crow caws and sings Her song of glory; your head will turn when I speak my truth and sing my song of war.

Blessed are the Women and Witches.

We are the Keepers of the Wild.

We are the Mistresses of War.

Author's note: This is not an attempt to compare the trauma endured by Military Service Women & Men around the world, please understand the metaphor here while also understanding that CPTSD is very real for civilians, too.

Morrigan and Her Crows

Paul Nixon

Where You're Supposed to Be

Molly Remer

What if staying safe and comfortable
is not where you're supposed to be?
What if it isn't supposed to be easy?
What if that raw edge
to your nerves,
that streak of pain on your skin,
that pang in your heart,
are the signs
that your soul is growing,
that you're on the verge
of an emergence
that would not be possible
without being
exactly where you are right now:
wild-eyed,
sharp-edged,
weary,
ragged,
fierce
and howling?

Listen
I am the Great Queen.
Fate whispers through my feathers
And winds through the songs of history.
I am she who transforms
I protect life with ferocity
And I walk freely with death.

Shriek Goddessy by Claire Dorey

A Shriek Goddessy

Claire Dorey

A guided meditation to help the modern 'gal' respond to the call of the Morrigan

Silk is not the best fabric to get tangled up in, especially in treetops.

Close your eyes and take three deep breaths: It is midnight and you are a human gyroscope, tumbling around in a turbulent nightmare, swivelling inside a parachute, plummeting toward the ground.

Half-awake now, to find your favourite silk pyjamas are twisted like a tourniquet. Anxious, contorted, heart pumping wildly and probably hallucinating, you adjust your eyes to the silvery moon light. You suspect you have been howling. Fear has cast a shadow across the walls of your bedroom, in the shape of a gigantic crow, flexing its wings. A She Wolf appears, creeping across the floor toward you, letting out a blood-curdling shriek. Could this be the call of the Morrigan?

Because you are familiar with the legend of a siren monster, in female form, a Metamorph, who roars into the lives of the 'summoned' via 'calling' dreams, you do not scream. You can't run because you are screwed up in your pyjamas, so shakily you ask, "Oh Goddess Morrigan why have you chosen me?"

The She Wolf rises up on her haunches and growls.

"I am Morrigan, sister of Badb, Macha, Banba, Fohla and Eriu, daughter of Ernmas, 'Great Queen', 'Phantom Queen', Triple Goddess of the cold Celtic North."

You are under her spell, captivated, although something seems off and you can't help thinking the Morrigan is reciting from a script.

"I'm a shape shifter, wolf, crow, eel – and folk lore says I protect armies and predict the outcome of war. When I appear, I come with a warning, for I am ruthless and revengeful, requiring stoic devotion. I have the power to haunt both you and your entourage. Priestesses and witches revere me, so show me some respect by preparing your alter and in return I'll use my Wolf Medicine to strip you back. I'll force you to face your fears. Then I'll dig out your buried strengths and wisdom and when I'm finished you'll be healed."

Terrified and intrigued, you are ready to let her leap into your shadow, because you've done a few workshops about being authentic, so you know that facing your demons and integrating the dark stuff is a sacred opportunity for healing, a chance to get in touch with your own Inner Goddess, well on the way to empowerment.

Morrigan shifts into human form, a striking woman, about the same age as you, with a lupine mane of shimmering black hair. She seems weary and sits down on the bed.

"I can't do this anymore," she yelps.

She's onto a different script now. It'll be impossible to stop her.

"I have not been slain by the writers of history because Morrigan mythology is infused with sexual politics, firmly on the side of male supremacy. I survived the interweaving of Pagan and Christian histories because my role as fearless Battle Totty,[16] to the tedious conflicts of the lords and masters, has been too important for them to get rid of me."

---

16 British slang, similar to 'hottie' in American English.

"My image is soooo old fashioned!" She wails.

"Let it out Morrigan," you whisper supportively – secretly resenting her for inserting her problems into your guided meditation.

"In the past the legend writers made me do ludicrous things with entrails and stupid stuff such as washing armour. Once they made me turn myself into a flock of ravens and fly about the battlefield, ordering me to take the dead away. I became an appendage of war. They demanded I jump into action with my armour on, whereas I actually prefer the kind of bravery where you strip yourself naked and surrender to vulnerability. Honestly I could smash my head against the wall, it has been that frustrating."

"My character has been demonised and sexualised, just as all Divine Feminine Power has been, since coming under Patriarchal control. I have remained typecast in this form because my existence, as part of the Zeitgeist, depended upon it. Now I'm completely exhausted and really need a break."

"Is there anything you like about yourself?" You ask.

"I like one-to-one visitations, like this one, as I'm a girl's girl," she replies, "and those who truly understand the Morrigan can gain great strength from me."

"I also like being a wolf," she barks, "Rewilding schemes are giving us She Wolves much better press, although we've been struggling for centuries. The truth is I am much more than I have been allowed to be. I'm tired of this role, it's been quite relentless. Don't you think it's time for a makeover? I'm going to shake things up – and you're going to help me!"

"Come strap on your crow wings and we'll fly back to pre-history where we will meet my 'Essence' – my purest of forms."

You are back in the meditation now, glad to be moving. Ever since early woman could walk upright, we've dreamed of flying and now you are swept up in the vortex, gliding through the sky with Morrigan, with a bird's eye view of the green fields of Ériu, through the swirling Irish mist. Thrilling in the acceleration, swooping in the thermals, you become a watcher. This is a magical flight.

You soar past the controllers and demonisers of women; past the paranoia and terror of the Witch Hunts; past dragons and dragon slayers; the Goddess denouncers; the whore labellers; the overwriting scribes; the biblical illusion and the bias of history.

From above, you witness the rise and fall of civilizations; Empire brutally expanding and contracting; refugees fleeing terror in boats. There are ant-sized soldiers, warlords, slaves and conquerors. Drought, mass extinctions, plague and famine ravage the landscape. You are unnerved by the dystopian paranoia; by suppression and control.

Dropping your wings, you slow your speed, for we are somewhere entirely different now and it is warmer and calmer here. Feeling safe, you take a deep breath. Perfume floats on the breeze. You taste honey. A swarm of bees guide your flight past subterranean temples; painted caves; sacred trees and wells; past megaliths and long barrows; past 'womb' tombs of the Matriarch and past the Grandmother Stones of the Paleolithic.

You fly along migration routes; through labyrinths; around spirals; over sacred symbols; past the Weavers and Spider Mothers. You swoop along rivers; past flocks of migrating water birds; witnessing the seasons; the harvest; the passage of time; the invention of the calendar, mathematics, geometry, astronomy and the alphabet. You float past vulva stones; lady bits; yoni temples, in honour of menstruation; goddess icons, doused in red ochre; libations, ether, kundalini, serpents and fire.

The Morrigan sets you down near a long house, in the heart of a nature sanctuary, next to a river bank. The sun is setting, cattle are grazing, children are playing. There is no hierarchy here. Women in trance are drumming and performing sacramental dance. Isis, Pythia, Melissae, Sophia, Medusa and Tiamet are here. The Wolf Goddesses, Leto and Skadi, scamper over to greet you. You feel your power rising as you connect with Wolf Medicine and begin to feel inseparable from all living things.

"Celtic folklore says I am the protector of rivers, livestock and people, however I am far more than that," bellows Morrigan, as you trot with the wolf pack, toward the river bank. "I am shaman, shape shifter, time traveller, tantric goddess, oracle, healer, spark of creation. I am Animist, connected to breath, life and spirit in all consciousness and the entire universe, including rocks, water, animals, plants, the weather, even all words."

"All Goddesses are creation and the circle of life," howl Skadi and Leto.

Hearing this you realise, all along, you had been waiting to experience the Divine Feminine, wishing it to become more obvious and dominant in the world.

"The circle of life is about renewal, life and death, creation and destruction," explains Morrigan. "All Goddesses, as life givers, have power over life and death, but legend has emphasised 'death and terror,' when it came to defining me, so I could be shoehorned into a belief system of domination and subordination, that is the hierarchy of Patriarchy, a system where nature is exploited and violence is an acceptable way of settling a dispute. They needed me to be terrifying, for they were suspicious of peace."

"Just as man hunted wolves to near extinction, they hunted the Goddess to take her power away. Legend could have written me out of history, killed me off, married me off, or turned me into a

59

man. Instead, they demonised me and just like the domestic dog, put me in captivity and set me to work. Anyway this is a long and epic story, there's volumes of it so right now I shan't be bothering you, with the existential crisis of the Goddess at the hands of the scribes!!"

You are invited to join the shamanic drummers who have formed a circle beside the river bank. It is Golden Hour. All Goddesses are here. The setting sun is low in the sky, fleetingly cradled between the horns of an Auroch, before slipping below the horizon. It's a Hathor-esque vision and your expectations are high, believing something significant will happen.

Thesis, Primordial Goddess of Creation, is tapping her Ankh on the side of a chalice, to draw everyone's attention.

"We have an urgent message for all receptive humanity," she announces. "The Earth is in crisis so we need to recruit Divine Warriors who are compassionate to Her suffering at the hands of humanity."

Day gives way to dusk, gold gives way to indigo, and Thesis continues.

"We need liberators committed to dismantling oppression; earth protectors; fuel activists and eco feminists. Men are, and I emphasize the word ARE, included in the term eco-feminist, this is the 3rd Millennium after all."

Thesis glances at her sister, Hydros, radiant Goddess of Mud, to double check that 5000 years immersed in the mineral rich, primordial sludge hasn't meant she missed the memo on men being feminists.

"Got it!" replies Hydros, adding, "It's a fair point, as sooo many men need encouragement to touch base with their repressed feminine sides. Plus they can get a teeny bit antsy when challenged, so best to be inclusive!"

A healing, pink Aura Borealis dances across the sky and Thesis continues her speech.

"We need peace envoys and environmentalists who can live in harmony with the Earth; sacred activists who share in the wonder of all living things and believe that inner freedom cannot exist without the well-being of the natural world."

She pauses, to check that everyone is listening, before making the 'big announcement.'

"As of now, all Goddesses will be stepping away from their 'legendary' roles and returning to their essential 'Essence' as Animists. You are tasked with enlisting realised beings and those whom we think can tune in with the consciousness of pulse and flow. It is time to reform the Matriarch."

Venus sparkles besides the full moon – the Grain Moon, in Aquarius – the moon of truth seeking and trusting in new journeys.

Sophia, Black Goddess, Mother of God and Goddess of Wisdom, speaks next.

"Just want to clarify that Matriarchy is not the same system as Patriarchy," she explains, looking directly at you. "It does not have a top down hierarchy, nor does it mean swapping a male figurehead for a female one. This is a common mistake."

A comet passes, far away in the galaxy and a jaguar wanders down to the water's edge, stooping to drink.

"Matriarchy is a holistic, interdependent, mother right, peaceful, Matrix system where everyone is equal. It doesn't exclude men by the way," says Sophia, her ebony skin glowing in the moonlight. "And in case you are wondering, Matrix is the late Latin word for Womb!"

Celestial energy bristles from the wolf pack, for after dark is when wolves are most magical. Neith, Warrior Goddess of Wisdom, War, Hunting and Weaving, ambles over. She reminds you of your games teacher – all jolly hockey sticks with ruddy cheeks.

"Unfortunately we can't change the current system by fighting it," she explains, "so the best way forward is to offer a better alternative. Like Morrigan I am tired of being an appendage of war. From now on I shall only be a Goddess and Warrior of Peace. The Earth depends upon us."

Neith squeezes your hand, "When you honour the Goddess we will walk beside you, every step of your journey."

Two days have passed. It's an icy morning and you are cycling along Sráid Nathair (Serpentine Street), wondering how many other women (and men) the Goddesses have recruited. Stopping at An Sean-Teach (The Old House) you notice the gate posts are constructed from recycled megaliths that once stood in a circle, 5000 years ago. Peering closer, you notice a spiral, carved into the stone, which you trace with your fingertips, unleashing the energy of Corra, the Irish Serpent Goddess, who once performed her Oraculor readings in a temple here, all those millennia ago. If you know where to look and what to look for you can find evidence, in a name, in a symbol, of the existence of the Matriarch.

A crow swoops in front of you and drops a piece of folded paper at your feet. You hear Morrigan's voice as you mouth the words written in the note, slipping back into trance, breath mingling with the cold Irish mist.

"Start your epic Goddess Eco Feminist Odyssey by recognising how great you are.

Be aware of your social conditioning and learn your own story.

Ask yourself, as I have done, what roles you have been shoehorned into, to meet the expectations of others.

Trust your intuition at all times.

Get in touch with your creativity, even if it's a few scribbles, as creative expression is divine energy.

Practice right speech and right action and act with compassion, kindness and gratitude.

Do not be wasteful, so cut your consumption and protect and connect with nature.

Cycle or walk when you can.

Please, please, pleeeeease reject processed food and live a life free of chemicals.

Do not add to animal suffering by eating meat.

Set up your Goddess alter, meditate and look after your body.

Align with others who raise your vibration to seek out sacred activists and learn all you can from them.

Listen to podcasts, read books, go to meetings, get involved with community.

Be nice to crows!

The path ahead will open up for you.

Most importantly, let the old and sick set the pace for the rest of the pack.

Remember, we Wolf Goddesses lead from the back!"

"PS. I'm not doing the nightmare visitations anymore, so call me on the mobile. Btw, aside from recruiting Divine Warriors, I'll be putting my Wolf Medicine to good use at the Wolf Conservation Centre, heading up their Rewilding Scheme." - XX - Smiley face - Love - Your Shriek Goddessy - Morrigan.

Fox Goddess

Alissa DeLaFuente

Offering

Alissa DeLaFuente

The contempt
& righteous anger
the hurts you gave to me
betrayal, injustice, misogyny
to hold like they were mine
she will gobble up
I will feed them to Her
bit by bit
bite by bite
a sacrifice on the altar
of becoming.

Raven

Alissa DeLaFuente

Answering The Morrigan's Call: Walking Beneath the Raven's Eye

Karen Storminger

I belong to the Morrigan and Blessed am I,
for I walk beneath the Raven's watchful eye.
I stand before her my soul stripped bare.
I face myself in her steely glare.
She is fierce, demanding of All or none.
Her challenge seeks truth, her sword cuts to the bone.
Within her embrace this heart is now Home.
Morrigan! Macha! Badb! Anu! She is named,
She is one, she is All! Come answer her Call!
Look into the darkness, let go of your fears.
In her embrace shed all of your tears.
Now is the time, her question is clear.
What do you stand for? What do you hold dear?
At the tip of her blade the challenge is set, DO NOT WAVER!
I stand before her, cold steel at my chest,
Gaze upon gaze
I speak the words, my truth, my Oath,
With the Morrigan's sword at my breast.
I belong to the Morrigan and Blessed am I,
For I walk beneath the Raven's watchful eye.

These are the words I was compelled to write after attending the first Morrigan's Call Retreat in June 2014.[17] These words still fill my heart and soul seven years later. They spur me on during my darkest days and ground me when I need it most. The Morrigan in my life has changed me, my path, solidified my purpose and opened the door for me to claim sovereignty over my own destiny.

---

17 The prayer at the beginning of the essay is titled "Morrigan's Prayer."

My path toward transformation began in the Spring of 2009. I was in a serious car accident. I was literally hit by a bus. Up until that point I was floundering spiritually. I knew I was going through the motions that year and I couldn't figure out which way I was being pulled. I was spinning my wheels in the mundane world and ignoring my own physical and spiritual needs.

Well, that just wouldn't do, so to send me a serious message I was hit quite hard with a Holy 2 x 4, only in the form of a bus. The car I was driving was completely totaled but I was lucky not to have been more seriously hurt or killed. That's when Morrigan stepped into my life. The presence was with me through my recovery and moving forward. It took me a little while (several years actually) and a lot of research to realize that presence was the Morrigan. Once I recognized this I started listening (you really have no choice with this Goddess) and in connecting to her, my life took a total 180-degree turn.

In June 2014, I was stressed out, knee deep in massage school, buried in bills and seriously depressed. I had spent the previous year dealing with the emotional turmoil that was my ex-husband as he faced death and dying. Truthfully, I had spent the last 30 years of my life dealing with him as both his wife and ex-wife. My life to that point was in constant high stress, survival mode. I had married young, had kids, struggled to get myself through college with babies in tow and eventually left a bad marriage. It was draining to say the least.

So, this is the state I was in when the opportunity to go to the first Morrigan's Call retreat was presented to me. I had been a practicing solitary for much of my life. I had mentors with whom I had corresponded with over the years, a small coven that came and went in the span of a year and had recently begun networking online with the Morrigu's Daughters. Having only known some of the people in this online group through the internet, I was contemplating going to the retreat which would be within driving distance for me. I hemmed and hawed over going for weeks. It was a terrifying thought to go off somewhere I didn't know with a group of people I didn't know. Especially when the last twenty-six years of my life had been about doing things for everyone else. I felt in my gut I should go, but my head had plenty of excuses.

I made the final decision to go and let my intuition lead me only two days before the retreat. I informed my children where I was going, and that cell service would probably be nonexistent there (we would be on a mountain in Massachusetts) and that they should call for help if I didn't return by Monday. This was my state of mind as I set off for Temenos in Massachusetts for the first Morrigan's Call retreat. I was going out into the woods to spend my weekend with a group of strangers. It turned out to be the best decision I made in my life.

I really had no idea what to expect. What I did know was that deep down within myself this was an experience I needed. My participation was important for me in that moment. A weekend of communing with nature, gaining a closer relationship with The Morrigan, and introspection. Little did I know how much introspection! Nor was I prepared for the depth and impact of the rituals planned for that weekend. I knew it would be a test for me in many ways. I had no idea how much of a test. To begin with, the area we were lodging at is a camping grounds up on a mountain in Massachusetts. No cell service, no electricity, no toilets, and spring water for showering. I chose to sleep in a tent not realizing; 1) It would be cold as hell in June at night, and 2) Bears. Others had wisely chosen to rent the cabins that were available or to get a cot in the main lodge house. This weekend was a test physically as well as spiritually. It began with hauling all our stuff from our cars up to the camping areas.

Then the park ranger gave a rousing pep talk about the safety rules on the mountain and what one should do if you thought you were being hunted by a bear. Yes, I said "hunted." Afterward, we set out as a group through the woods to the temple. There, prayers, dedications, and offerings to the Morrigan in her different aspects were given. This for me was pivotal. It was in this moment that I felt it, that sudden realization that I was indeed in the right place at the right time. Over the course of the rest of the weekend one thing built upon the next, each individual ritual was more profound than the one before it, all culminating on the last day to the overwhelming feeling of belonging. I had for the first time in many years found kindred souls. I had found my center; my own spiritual spark was reignited. In the woods, on a mountain in Massachusetts with a group of strangers I had answered the call of The Morrigan.

That weekend was an ending and a beginning for me. In taking that trip, making that leap out of my comfort zone, I had taken the first step on a new path. I was making the conscious decision to leave my old life behind and try something new. This was the catalyst for a myriad of changes in the following years. I became friends with several people in that group of strangers and began working with them and others in group settings for ritual. I made changes in my attitudes toward myself, my health, my career and really began to build toward creating the life I wanted for myself.

Eventually I changed jobs and moved to another state to start an entirely new life on my own. My adult children stayed in the state we had always lived in and began their own lives as well. I met someone new and am now in a much healthier relationship. I am living the life I had always envisioned and wished for myself now. Every step of the way in this journey The Morrigan has been at my back, at my side and in my heart. My connection with this Goddess has inspired and challenged me. She has taught me to see my own worth and never settle for less than what is rightfully mine.

When I think of the Morrigan I think of the many aspects of this Goddess and how she shifts seamlessly from one to another depending on her need and intent. Each aspect distinctly different and individual, yet still all Morrigan. When I connect with Macha, I am connecting with the characteristics of hard work, self-sufficiency, self-confidence, and self-determination. Macha claims what is hers, fights for what is right, and has no issues with telling those who have wronged her exactly how they will reap the consequences of their actions. In her stories and under her guidance, I have learned hard lessons. Most importantly to stand up for myself and claim what is rightfully mine. Badb, to me, is the crack of lightening on a warm summer night. She is the sudden realization of the inevitable. Harsh and hard at times, but only when it is needed – most likely to get your full attention. She is the inner work, the emotional work, the letting go, ripping away of all that weighs you down.

I have dealt with some painful things and given them over to Badb. Once I had come to terms with letting that happen, she has gifted me innumerably as one of her own. Badb was the bus in my life, after which I faced a lot of pain and loss before I could transform. Anu is the most grounding for me. My connection to Anu came only recently in the last few years. Anu was here to greet me in my new home, my new life. Once I had stepped on the path, done the work, fought the battle and claimed my due, Anu has been there to show me what stability, peace and growth can be in my life. She reminds me to stop fighting small all the time. To live in peace and grow in abundance and to rest so I am ready when I'm called to stand up and enter a worthy battle.

About 5 years after answering the Morrigan's Call and accepting her presence in my life, I was gifted a healing session with a local energetic healer. During my session, of course the Morrigan was present. This healer saw me with black wings enveloping me like a feathered cloak. She also said something which struck me significantly:

"You hold your pain, fear and anger inside you. But you do something different with it. You store it in your spine. You transform these emotions which could destroy a person who simply held them and stuffed them down within themselves. Instead, you have used them to forge a sword. When a situation occurs that would cause fear or uncertainty, you remain calm and reach behind your back and draw from these stored emotions a weapon. You use it to cut through the truth of the matter."

This for me was further confirmation that The Morrigan has always been with me. This Goddess has profoundly influenced and inspired me to transform my life and claim my own sovereignty in this world. I am not the same woman I was when this journey began. I know there is much more growth and change to come in my journey with The Morrigan, as I walk beneath the Raven's watchful eye.

A Blessing for the Brave and Tender

Molly Remer

May you be brave
in your devotion
and bold
in your noticing.
May you be audacious
in your hope
and courageous
in your listening.
May you be stubborn
in your joy
and tender
in your determination.
May you hold yourself
and others
with fierce trust
and ferocious,
wild
love.

The Hunter

Andrea Redmond

The Shining Ones

Molly Remer

This is for the shining ones.
Incandescent with purpose,
alive with passion,
aflame with calling.
The bright,
the inspired,
the blazing.
Those who burn fiercely
without apologizing
for their fire.
May you trust your light.
May you honor the shining.
May you continue to glow,
unafraid,
unashamed,
undimmed.

Birth, Death and Rebirth—
How The Morrigan Restored My Sovereignty

A personal essay by Dr Karen Ward

Growing up in Dublin, Ireland, The Morrigan's warrior feats did not grace my childhood bedtime stories. It wasn't until I was in my early thirties that I heard tell of this fearsome creature – the Irish equivalent of Kali, the Destroyer of the East. I was intrigued yet repelled, fascinated but unable to relate to her in my cosy middle-class life of privilege and busyness.

However, as is often the way of The Morrigan, she had her beady crow eye on me, unbeknownst to my wild and naive heart. Years passed and having kissed many frogs I finally met my prince. We enjoyed our honeymoon blissful union telling ourselves that we had plenty of time for baby making. The Morrigan, waiting in the wings, knew differently. At first, we assumed that all we needed was the rhythm of my cycle to attune to our hopeful intentions but about to turn forty, time was not on my side. As a practitioner of Celtic Shamanism, I had collected totems of new life and was fully convinced that, having had a charmed existence so far, this too would come to pass.

The Morrigan is revered as holding the archetypal energies of the triple aspect of birth, death and rebirth. In the past she has been much maligned and feared as a Death Goddess but I was to discover that she brings so much more to our consciousness. Eventually I answered her insistent call and came to know the eternal cycle of birth, death and rebirth is a continuum and that this powerful Goddess would teach me at a visceral level, exactly what that meant.

As I yearned for the birth of my motherhood, I told our families and friends. I charted my Moontime rhythms but month after month brought the red tide of my dreams receding on the shore of disappointment and sadness. I tried to call in Goddess Brigid, the midwife and Matron Saint of babies but it was The Morrigan who visited my nighttime reveries again and again. I had two miscarriages – the memory of one so vivid in the depths of Winter as we travelled to my ancestral home of Derry. I remember the excitement of leaving full of hope and joy and arriving to the cold, dark, feeling of despair. Birth was not to be. It took me a full three years to acknowledge this fact.

I fought the dawning realisation. I ignored the signs and there were plenty. I prayed to every deity I knew and still The Morrigan sat by me... waiting. I had to descend into her proverbial Rathcroghan Cave to grieve. There I felt Badb, her sister's shadowy presence as though supporting me from the Underworld. In the cool earthy darkness, I shed tears of sorrow, shame, fear, frustration and finally relief. As I crawled out, we set a fire and held by my man, I sacrificed the baby clothes and symbols of motherhood to the hungry flames as the crows wheeled in the sky above me, dawn breaking. I howled wolf-like as part of my soul broke that day.

And yet... somehow, I knew that there was more. The Morrigan, warrior of the heart, was not finished with me. As the days turned to months, I began to welcome her invitation to relish an internal movement as new hope began to stir deep within after the release of death. From the pendulum of lethargy and inchoate sadness, there came an energetic catapult as though towards the living vibrancy of Summer leaving the death of WInter's cold breath. She helped me shapeshift to gain perspective and fly high over my destiny path. The Great Queen revealed that like the Earth, I too could be reborn to the abundance of my sovereignty as a woman. This time it was Macha, her sister in the Upperworld who supported me as I journeyed to Tír na nÓg, the Land of the Ever Young, to glimpse the brightness of my soul journey and how this epic voyage of birth and death would lead to my rebirth as a wiser, sovereign version of myself. This experience would serve me well to bring to the wider world that there are many ways to be a woman and specifically a woman in her full and joyous power.

The Morrigan, the outward incarnation of this powerful triskel of Goddesses, is the least known, feared and understood of the Celtic Goddesses and yet, I recognise that she is the one that affects us all at key times in our lives. Her energy is subtle yet can be powerfully wild – it all depends on how we personally view the birth, death, rebirth cycle. She continues to help me know that I must release old ways and patterns to create space for the new to grow. How can I possibly manifest my life destiny if I am mired and stuck in the past? The mighty Morrigan assists me to become aware of old cycles and break through them completely. Her energy is subtle yet can be powerfully wild – it all depends on how we personally view death. If we are afraid then we may view death with dread and loathing. However, if we are unafraid then we will live life to the full and recognise and relish rebirth. When we answer her calling, she will assist us to overcome. Finally, I came to know and understand The Morrigan Great Queen in all her glory with gratitude, respect and love.

Rise of The Morrigan

Paul Nixon

A Seed Dream

Molly Remer

Let the sun dry your tears
and soak passion back into
your bones.
Let the wind sweep through you
and leave you cleansed and renewed.
Let the earth receive your woes;
sink your roots deep
and draw up the support
that is all around you.
Feel the small spark
of desire at your core
kindle into life,
a burning ember of purpose
that cannot be extinguished.
If your hope is seeping away,
hold onto it,
you need it.
If your caring is fading
into nothing,
refuse to give it up,
it is worth tending.
If you have lost sight of your "why"
ask for it,
and listen carefully to the answer.
If your devotion is wavering
and you are standing uncertainly
on the wobbly edges
of a changing life,
inspire it,
nourish it fiercely,
like a precious seed
that can grow a new world.

Sometimes

Jessica Johnson

Sometimes, my goddess humbles me. She shows me glimpses of the path I'm going to have to walk, and I know she's going to put me through a lot. I'm talking transformations akin to walking through fire, becoming remade. I *will* suffer, but I, or a part of me, will be transformed in the process.

Other times, I feel held, even cradled by my goddess, for she is also a mother as well as being a goddess of death. She knows not all things can be borne with a stiff upper lip and a bandage, but requires some love and gentle reminders about what I've come through and what I'm capable of.

And sometimes, when deep down I know I'm acting like a sullen teenager trying to put off the inevitable, she's an ice queen, refusing to tolerate my behavior. In these times all it takes is one good rebuff for me to smarten up and assume the warrior stance. In all of these moments though, I know that The Morrigan is with me.

She *is* the fire that I must walk through. I sacrifice the layer of myself that is dead and serves me no longer. It is difficult to face The Morrigan in her death goddess guise, to sacrifice a part of *me* to her, even if it's a part of me that I've outgrown and don't need any longer. But, just like in the end we can't take our things with us, I can't take this old version of me any further, and I must walk the coals, feeling the old me burn away. It leaves me raw and vulnerable to the world, ready to face the new...

Ultimately what I feel for the Morrigan is love. I don't feel her motherly side often, but when I do it's almost enough to stop my heart with love. The truly beautiful and amazing things that I get to see and experience when this side of her is revealed to me is breathtaking. Just as fierce as she is in her warrior aspect, she is intense in her love too. This is the side of my goddess that I think is the least seen or understood by outsiders. She is so often depicted as the warrior, the harbinger of death, the Phantom Queen, that you don't get to see that she is also a goddess of the earth and fertility.

I am most proud of my goddess when she's in her warrior guise. The strength that radiates from her, it's awe-inspiring, and not just a little bit intimidating. When I see Warrior Morrigan I know the road before me will not be easy, but I also know not to worry, for I have the world's best warrioress at my side. Her strength and righteous anger is *my* strength and righteous anger. She comes to my defense, but she also comes as my teacher, showing how to block, not give ground, and where to strike the most effective blows.

People have remarked to me that they are amazed at times by my strength, but I think a part of me has known all along that I've had a little help, and I've been guided by an amazing teacher. Though I've only been a daughter of the Morrigan in name for about five years, I've known she's been my guide in my heart for most of my life.

The Morrigan is a fierce and powerful goddess, and over the years her name has been warped and twisted, made synonymous with trickery and evil. But if she plays tricks with you, it is a lesson. If she scares you, it is a tough-love call-to-action. If she intimates you, it is a reminder not to bow down to anyone when your boundaries are tested. She doesn't want to dominate you, she wants to *empower* you. The question is, are you to no longer be tamed? Are you ready to fight?

Once you let The Morrigan in, you, and your life, will no longer be the same. You will be tested. You will be held to some higher expectations. You will cry, you will scream, you will grieve. But you will also love and be loved, you will dance, you will smile, you will laugh, you will cry out in ecstasy and in joy. You will *live* like you have never lived before.

So, she asks you... are you ready? Are you ready to look death in the face and see your shadow selves up close and then come back to life again? Are you ready to see the most beautiful things imaginable? Just like these paradoxes reside in her, they reside in you too. So, she asks you...

Are you ready?

Morrigan

Laura Cameron

Finding the Strength to Love and Re-Claiming My Sovereignty

Deborah A. Meyerriecks

It is an act of love to allow yourself to receive love and be loved without expectations, rules, or limitations. I still strive to continue my personal shadow work to actively heal from traumas not often spoken. Traumas which led to allowing myself to be chosen by the wrong partners, manipulated, and hurt. Traumas that left me feeling the need to perpetuate relationships that were harmful or damaging because failure in a relationship was a failure of self. Learning to let myself be loved as the other person is capable, taking the time to learn their method of communicating their love even when it is so completely different from what I understand and know how to communicate myself is a sheer act of courage.

After all, have we not been told how love is a battlefield? It shouldn't be. Some of us are either refugees of that war or suffering the damage of being in a struggle for survival. When you have been significantly hurt in the name of love since childhood, when that trauma led to a pattern of abusive relationships, and that in turn fostered an unwillingness to openly communicate because personal honestly can be used against you, we shut down and build walls of protection. When love is a battlefield, it's hard to tell in the melee who is friend and who is foe. Who is an ally? Who is a partner who truly has your back? Who is willing to put themselves at risk by guarding you as they trust you to guard them as well? Who is just looking for the easy way to self-gratification and not concerned with who they hurt in the process?

Opening myself to The Morrigan, learning my own strength and capabilities and my own sovereign worth, is enabling me to take a "We first" mentality in my current partnership.

After I heard the Call of the Morrigan and began to attend Her retreats I soon learned the nameless Goddess that had been with me and supported me in my work was Herself. The more I learned about Her and took daily time to get to know Her, the more I understood that this was my truth. What I was coming to understand should have been obvious all along. I wasn't a Warrior, I was a medic. Yet this Battle Queen stood with me while I did the work of healing myself and gave me the insight to be able to support others though their own fights. One thing I came to understand is that everyone is fighting a battle of their own. The more She supported me in helping others in my work as a NYC EMT, the more I learned to apply the same work to myself. I learned there can be strength in vulnerability when you have the personal strength to reclaim and hold on to your personal power.

After my 1st annual retreat at The Call of the Morrigan, I learned to stand up for myself with kindness. I had been living with someone who was a friend but not exactly a partner in love. The longer we tried to force it, the worse it got. Being enabled to see this clearly, I initiated talks. We decided we needed to dissolve our handfasting. We are better friends now than we ever were before because I was able to be clear about what I needed while still being kind. Kind is not always nice and that's OK. In the following year, an old on-again off-again paramour tried to be on again. He never had time when I needed or wanted him. I knew it was limiting me from continuing my personal healing. After 20 years, I found the self-worth to tell him goodbye. That's something I only say once. It's final. It was scary and I needed to make myself angry to do it but I got it done for myself soon after I attended my 2nd Call of the Morrigan retreat. That was the year She claimed me as one of Her priests.

That Summer I felt myself becoming more myself than I had in decades. For the Autumn Equinox I was going to release myself from needing to be in a romantic partnership while stepping fully into service as the community priestess I'd become. Something else happened. I was invited to a semi-public ritual where a friend was leading for her first time. Another friend lit a candle dedicated to The Morrigan and placed it on its usual shelf on a wall, a few feet from the ceiling. We were given rice paper to write what we would banish. In turn we would dissolve it in a cauldron of water while stirring widdershins with our anthem or wand or finger. I hadn't written anything until I approached the altar. When I got there, I wrote "limitations." I banished limitations. I felt an energy around me gain excitement. When we all took a turn and were back in circle, tea lights were passed around to all of us. We were to pass the flame from one lit candle to the next in circle together. While doing this we would silently or out loud state what we were drawing in for balance. When it was my turn, I invoked Bliss. I heard an intake of breath behind me with a sound that was like one makes when pleasantly surprised. Like, 'oooh, she did do that!"

Finally, we were invited to give something to the acting priestess to bless in ritual. I took off my necklace with a triquetra charm and gave it to her. When I returned to my place in circle, I felt something sharp stab me low under my right scapula. The candle dedicated to The Morrigan flared up and scorched a black mark onto the ceiling. When I looked at my charm in my hand, the silver was black. I rubbed it thinking it was just lamp black from the candle flame used to bless it with fire. It remained black. I heard a voice in my head telling me "Offering accepted, what was asked for will be granted." With what sounded like a chuckle I also heard "be ready."

After that circle I felt drained yet elated. Someone behind me noticed my cloak was cut into a perfect Sargent's strip, a double chevron cut. When I took of my cloak, there was dried blood on my shirt and I had a small cut where I felt I'd been stabbed earlier.

Less than a week later, I was introduced to my current partner in love. A week after that he texted me in all caps that I was worth it all, to stop doubting myself and my self worth. I don't recall what I said, but he told me "Welcome home." I instantly had thoughts that the stab during ritual was The Morrigan, creating a chip in my icy armor of protection because she knew I was strong enough not to need it up full time anymore. In that moment though, as I felt my protective barrier shatter and fall, I felt cold, exposed and vulnerable. My partner texted the same words I heard Herself in my head telling me. I was strong enough to not need it. That no one was going to be able to get close enough to me with it. They both reminded me that I have always been strong enough but it's up to me to get comfortable with my own strength.

In the months that became years to follow, I have learned that you cannot control love. You cannot control a relationship. All parties are needed and communication is a skill we need to constantly be willing to learn together. The silence speaks volumes when you understand how to listen. It's not always negative. Sometimes it's because they are comfortable and feel safe and secure in your love as they feel you are in theirs.

It doesn't matter how many people loved you or said they did but really didn't love you in the past. In the present moment, each day, what matters is the love you are getting, how that makes you feel, and whether you are able to participate in that exchange. It's scary at times. Courage isn't about not being afraid. Often, courage is being afraid and doing something anyway. I was prepared to block this type of love from my life so I could feel safe. Thus, I'd be able to focus on my work of service. It's sometimes all too easy to declare oneself unlovable. After decades of trying to hold on to the wrong relationships and trying to make them work even when it's apparent they never were meant to last is not uncommon.

The time when we were planning our first weekend away, I made a decision about who I am and how I want to love going forward. I told him that if after we spent that time together he realized I am not his person all I wanted was his honesty. In weeks we had been together already I discovered a feeling of just being happy. If our relationship ended before it really started, nothing could take that time of happiness from me. I could diminish it but decided I would not do that to myself anymore. We met through an online mutual friend and we lived in different states yet I never felt closer to anyone before we were introduced.

It's almost 4 years. We are still together. It's been challenging in that I have needed to learn how to communicate honestly and listen to what was being said and not listen from a place of trauma and fear of not being good enough. Last year for a variety of reasons I decided it was time to sell my house. Discussing it together, I made the decision to rent a house near where he lives and works. It was time to see if this long distance relationship could work in person. Of course, nothing is ever easy. The key is to not internalize the difficulties and make it about your mutual love and respect for each other. It isn't always a sign that things aren't meant to be. Often it means you have more scars that need care to heal. We have limited time and he has a multitude of family and work obligations, made only worse due to the current pandemic. Again, I had the conversation with him about whether or not we would last together and how I would feel. Sure, if we don't survive the test of time and realize we aren't meant to live together, I'm going to be sad. That will be temporary and it won't take away from the general feeling of happiness being loved this much has brought me. I told him that if we can't find a way to live together I still can accept his love and love him back. I have days it's beyond not easy. Believe me. I do know that I have a Warrior Queen of a Goddess on my side and at my back. She reminds me that I am not defined by what others did to me in the past. I am whole. I am strong. I am worthy.

Even when at times it is difficult to understand, I try to refrain from making snap judgments about what an exchange or lack of one means. Understanding requires compassion and kindness. It requires patience. Through mutual understanding, we grow. Generally, it takes time for a wounded heart to heal. To learn to trust again. To be willing to be loved at the risk of being broken again. I feel like with The Morrigan, I got a strong push into the deep end. A sink or swim situation. She only offers her sword to those who are strong enough to wield it. One dream I had with Her when I was still learning to be open and be in love with my partner, was particularly telling. I was standing on the bank of a river when She beckoned me to Her. Without warning, She pushed me under the water and held me down. I watched as I dissolved and flowed away with the current. Standing up, She looked at me still on the riverbank. "Good," She said. "You didn't drown. You have work to do." I turned and saw myself standing a distance away on a slight hilltop. My partner with me. I remember hearing in my head, "It's a harder climb than it looks but you're up for it. Now get going. You have work to do."

The Morrigan is not by any means a love goddess. She is not a healer. She is the Warrior Herself. Sovereign Queen and Goddess of Battle. Especially in Macha. I am Her Priest.

It's only natural that a goddess of personal sovereignty and a goddess of the battle would lend Her sword and strength to those who are willing to get up and try and try again each day. No matter that their personal battle breaks them down. No matter if they lose their fight. The honor is in the showing up and trying. Stepping into the pain and stepping up for themselves. She was there to empower me through my own fight. She stayed with me while I found my way home to myself. It is in Her honor that I will not close myself off ever again. I have learned my own strength and I am no longer afraid of it.

One of my gifts has always been the ability to be present for others. To actively see them exactly where they were in that moment. To listen with compassion and kindness. Reminder: Kindness is not always nice. It's real and it's honest.

The Morrigan empowered me to turn that ability back toward myself, enabling me to live present in each new moment. To maintain an understanding of where I have been that could be affecting how I am reacting in that moment. To pause and choose how I'd prefer to respond. All with an awareness of where I am going and where I want to be in my future. All while remaining actively present for myself, what I'm thinking, how I am feeling, and what I need. More than anything else, that has enabled the deepest moments of productive self-shadow work. It led to a deeper understanding of why I reacted a certain way before which enabled me to choose how I'd respond in the current moment.

My work with The Morrigan has given me strength to heal myself which has led to a calm grace in conflict befitting a sovereign who is recognized without need for announcement. Accepting Her Sword was my first step in learning to love and heal myself.

Ravenspirit

Laura Cameron

Badass Warrior Goddess

Sharon Smith

I love a Badass Warrior Goddess
With a big-ass sword.
Especially when she knows how to use it
To slice and dice through patriarchal flesh and bone,
To break through androcentric rock and stone
And let women, beaten down by patriarchal men
Know they will never, EVER walk alone again.

I used to be a mousey gal,
Pushed around by abusive men,
Thinking I was "lesser than,"
A never-ending cycle of
"Try, try again and again and again"—
And for what? So I could be called
A cunt, a whore, a twat...

Struggling, day in and day out
But never quite getting there;
Never quite good enough.
"Daughter of Eve" and all.
Responsible for "the Fall."
Fuck that shit! I've heard the Call
Of the Baddest Ass Warrior Goddess
Of them All!

The Morrigan is her name
My Twin (Sister) Flame.
Funny... because I feared her
Before I revered her;
Her Darkness frightened me
Before it enlightened me.

I cringed and cowered
Before I became empowered.

But she took me through her Dark School
Taught me not to be a fool,
Taught me how to get my shit together
Grow my wings and fly in any weather...
She showed me the value of the Night;
How everything is not all "Love and Light"
How sometimes we must take a righteous stand
Warrior up and repossess the stolen land.

I learned from Her that Darkness
Can be a Healer and Revealer
Like a Mother's Womb to hold me,
A place of Transformation to mold me
Crack my ribs and break my bones
Rip my flesh and grow me some stones,
Yeah, Baby! Great Big Balls of Steel
The Morrigan taught me what it means
To be authentically real...

That's what she showed me
This Raven-eyed, Ebony Queen,
Shredder of Lies and
Destroyer of False Dreams;
Revealer of Ancient Truth
And Sacred Feminine Ways;
And I'll gladly follow Her
Though dark be the nights,
And darker yet the days;
Glad that I answered the Call
Of the Baddest Ass Warrior Goddess
Of them all.

Note from author: The Morrigan brings out the Wild Warrior Woman in my soul. From Her kick-ass, no-apologies-given persona I draw a tremendous amount of courage and strength... and for that, I am deeply grateful to this Celtic Dark Goddess. She is one of my favorites!

The Morrigan Mask

Lauren Raine

From the *Masks of the Goddess Project*, which ran from 1998-2019.

Eel Kundalini, St Patriarch
and the Wide Sargasso Sea

Claire Dorey

"When St Patrick – St Patriarch – drove the snakes out of Ireland he forgot about the EELS! E-v-e-r-y-o-n-e FORGETS about the EELS! And it is this aspect of myself that I want to talk about."
-The Morrigan

"Ever since I've been invoking the Goddess I've noticed that wherever there is a serpent, there is hidden knowledge waiting to be revealed. I hadn't really considered Eels. The Eel is an overlooked aspect of the Morrigan so I felt compelled to investigate. She steered me to a cache of dark history that shouldn't be forgotten." -The Author

To understand the Eel is to contemplate the moonlight as it falls on water and what lies beneath. Moonshine amplifies the magic that is water – the elixir of life. Streams, rivers and oceans ebb and flow with the cleansing, purifying, renewing, intoxicating, maddening, trance-inducing, portal opening phases of the moon. The domain of the Eel is embedded in the emotionally charged water vortexes and conduits that sustain the Earth.

Boundless energies govern these cycles. Water vapour is swept into the sky from the surface of the oceans. Clouds travel back to the land and release rain over the hills and mountains forming streams and rivers that nourish the earth, which flow back into the oceans. Legend says the Tuatha Dé Danann – the folk descended from the Goddess Danu, including the Morrigan – arrived in Ireland in dark clouds of mist and landed on the mountains. The primordial essence and electrically charged ancestral wisdom of the Eel is born from these vast moon, water and memory cycles. This is an intrinsically Feminine system.

It is Spring. I am in Ireland and I am straddling the muddy bank of a meandering stream, one foot in the water, one in the sludge, collecting wild garlic. This tiny patch of indigenous woodland, growing along the twisting creek, is carpeted with the frondescence of wild garlic. It is raining. As the rain hits the undergrowth the medicinal aroma of Allium is released. It mingles with petrichor and the soft scent of moss that clings to the north facing branches of the age-wizened trees.

It's very healing here. Tuning into the wisdom of the trees and the stream in flow – to the nourishment that is the Goddess – I am not at all surprised when the Morrigan appears.

She's lying in the mud, legless, leaden grey, mucous covered and slippery. The Morrigan is in her Eel form and she is half submerged, literally up to her vestigial elbows, in the silt that coats the river bank. Her face is pre-historic and she has a double row of razor sharp teeth. A blade-like fin runs the length of her spine. So far I can see five feet of her, but I think there may be more of her, hidden beneath the sludge!

"Do not believe the accounts that say there weren't any snakes in Ireland," hisses the Morrigan. "Of course there were! Will you just look at the Celtic knot; or listen to tales of the Corra, the great serpent Goddess, swallowing St Patriarch; or ponder why our Druid sisters carved images of Her into the standing stones."

The Morrigan is uncoiling her body, heaving herself onto the river bank. She is huge, at least twelve feet long.

"When Ireland was connected to Doggerland there were snakes." She bellows. "When Ireland was covered in ancient forest there were plenty of snakes – wisdom snakes – and our ancestors honoured them. Then St Patriarch drove the Corra out. Of course, the term 'drove out' is 'zealot wash' for 'hunted them down and exterminated them.' It was a blood bath. A witch hunt for snakes.

That was when female wisdom, inseparable from the 'mysteries' of the serpent, retreated underground... sort of! I say 'sort of' because St Patriarch forgot about the Eels! He forgot to drive us Eels out of Ireland."

Buds of horns protrude from her forehead as the Morrigan becomes emotional.

"Our Divine Eel wisdom is still here, camouflaged by silt and sadly it is often overlooked."

"To understand the tenacity of the Eel you must understand what happened to our serpent sisters," explains the Morrigan. "Ever since Gilgamesh, the patriarch have murdered and dismembered the serpent, or stolen Her sacred knowledge, claiming it as their own."

"Asclepius killed a snake and stole Her medicinal knowledge. Apollo murdered Gaia's serpent protectors and built his temple upon Her temple. Poseidon raped Medusa and She got blamed for it. Perseus murdered Medusa and the world declared him a hero. Lilith, Eve and Sophia were all silenced and demonised for practicing Serpent 'Knowing.' The legs of the Wisdom Serpent were hacked off before She was cast out of Eden. When St Patriarch murdered the Corra, destroying the morale of the Druids, he was declared a saint. When Theodosius the Roman emperor terminated the Pythia, dismantling the generations of conduits to Earth wisdom, the word 'Great' was added to his name. Hercules joined the ranks of the hero-murderer, hero-rapist archetype when he slaughtered the Hydra, the eight headed, serpentine daughter of the sea serpent Echidna. Echidna was daughter of primordial sea serpent Goddess Ceto, who was also Medusa's mother. Ceto's mother was Gaia, primordial Earth Goddess and mother of all life."

Making a link with Celts and ancient Greece is valid. In one legend, the sea nymph Galateia, the Goddess and spirit of the sea, was the mother of the Galatis (Gallic Celts).

"Do you see where I'm going with this?" Asks the Morrigan, using her visceral strength to rise up my arm, so her eye is level with my eye. Her breath is putrid.

"The patriarch," I whisper, recoiling slightly, "feared the cycles of fertility, immortality and oracular magic of serpent wisdom?"

"Y-e-e-e-s but don't you see what I'm getting at?" urges the Morrigan. "Look at me properly. Where am I?"

"You are on a river bank, covered in duckweed. You just emerged from the silt." I reply.

"E-X-A-C-T-L-Y!" she shrieks, "and you don't get much more primordial than that!"

"In this aspect I am connected with generations of mystical Ophidian creatures who have a direct lineage to the Earth... AND to the Ocean! What's more I have successfully hidden from the patriarch!"

The Morrigan is calmer and her horns have subsided. I can see the outline of a human face beginning to form.

"In my Eel form I am Earth, underworld, ocean and rain. I carry the wisdom of Earth Mother Gaia, who was born of mud and Goddess Danu, who travelled as mist. I am descended from generations of primordial sea monsters and their serpent daughters. This power is always present, hidden in plain sight, waiting to be discovered by those who look."

"I travel across the sea, and up the river mouth, from salt water to fresh. I can walk across land and go deep in the crevices of the earth. I can be a frightening warrior from the netherworld, who fights invaders, or a caring sister who caresses and soothes the process of birth. I travel far and wide but always return to the place I was born."

The soft Spring rain is a nourishing rain. I don't feel wet. I feel uplifted! We are sitting side-by-side and the Morrigan has taken on a half-human, half-Eel form. Actually she looks like a mermaid. Her face is otherworldly, pale, luminescent. She has enormous, myopic eyes and her hair cascades over her breasts like seaweed. Her hips curve into grey slipperyness and I'm pleased that to note that her breath is now fragrant!

"I can read your mind," declares the Morrigan. "You find the Eel to be a slightly distasteful creature."

"Um," I reply. I have no words beyond 'Um' to describe what I think.

"No worries," teases the Morrigan. "Um is a good word!"

Quite some time passes. We sit shoulder-to-shoulder. deep in thought, watching mist swirl above the water. A minnow jumps to catch a fly, breaking through the surface of the water, which is as smooth and clear as glass. Occasionally I receive a gentle electric shock, that gives me goosebumps, as the Morrigan's skin touches mine.

"These sparks are Eel Kundalini," explains the Morrigan. "Trust in the awakening process of the divine Eel Goddess."

We fall back into silence and I contemplate the stream and the path it takes toward the ocean.

"Where does this water flow to?" I ask.

"It flows to my birth place," replied the Morrigan. "All Eels are born in the Sargasso Sea. All the Eels in Ireland have swum huge distances across the Atlantic Ocean. We return to the Sargasso Sea to spawn and die. This is our great cycle of birth, death and rebirth, of disintegration and regeneration. Before we die, we become beautiful. We light up the ocean with chromatic flashes – the divine sparks of our creation. That is part of Eel Kundalini."

I google the Sargasso Sea and discover it is a unique eco-system and area of calm within the Atlantic Ocean, that is enclosed in a behemoth whirlpool of rotating currents. It's an oval mass of emotionally charged, deep blue water that is like nowhere on Earth. It has no fixed position and undulates and drifts. The nearest landmass is the East coast of North America and it is 'cupped' by the Bahamas, Cuba and Haiti. The Bermuda Triangle lies within it. Africa is far to the South East and Ireland is far away, to the East.

"I have read the Wide Sargasso Sea," I tell the Morrigan.
The novel, written from an anti-colonial perspective, is about the problem of racial identity on the sugar plantations, in the West Indies, when slavery ends. It was written by Dominican feminist author, Jean Rhys, in response to Charlotte Brontë's novel, Jane Eyre.

"I didn't realise Mr Rochester's first wife was locked up, when they returned to England, not because she was mad, as declared in Jane Eyre, but because she was 'Creole.'"

"You are right to pay homage to our novel writing sisters, who offer a variety of historical perspectives," says the Morrigan. "Let me tell you my story."

"The Sargasso Sea was right in the path of the transatlantic slave trade triangle," explains the Morrigan, flipping her ophidian tail, with an air of sadness.

"For centuries the Sirens, Harpys, Mermaids and Selkies had been relaying horrific news of what was happening there."

"They were also concerned about the trees, plundered from the Irish forests. The Celts worshipped in groves of Oak trees. The mountains, bogs, streams and trees were alive with spirits. For millennia invaders harvested the forests. Roman Christians cut the trees down to build churches and monasteries and the English colonisers decimated the forests because the 'resistance' hid there. Irish wood was used for the roof of Salisbury Cathedral and to fuel the industrial revolution. They used a lot of the wood for ship building. It was a holocaust for trees."

"Three hundred or so years ago I set out from St Brigid's church in Kildair. I swam along the Morrel River, into the River Liffey and out into open water at Dublin. In the Celtic Sea I started to follow a ship, built from Irish wood, as it left the Bristol Channel, all the way to the Pepper Coast in Africa. When the galleon docked, guns were unloaded and chattel slaves, yoked together at the neck, were forced onboard," The Morrigan's voice cracked. "It was terrible," she wailed.

"I followed the English ship, built of Irish wood, full of African Slaves, as it sailed across the Atlantic to the Sargasso Sea, the birth place of Eels."

"What happened next was pure genocide. The sick and dying and those too weak to be sold as slaves, were thrown overboard."

"The ship sailed on to Hispaniola, where the chattel slaves were dragged to the market, whilst the clipper was packed with rum and sugar. The ship then sailed up the coast of North America stocking up with whale oil and cotton and then back to England, where that cargo was replaced with more guns and the ship sailed back to Africa, to repeat the whole diabolical cycle. British slave ships took 42,000 of the 80,000 Africans transported, chained and shackled, across to the 'New World' each year. More than a million are thought to have died en route."

"I couldn't follow the ship anymore. I was an emotional wreck, exhausted, so I stopped in Hispaniola, where the slaves hid me in their bunkhouse and Maman Brigitte, the rum drinking Goddess, nursed me with Vodou, alcohol and chili pepper."

"Is Maman Brigitte the counterpart of St Brigid?" I ask.

"It's true that Haitian Vodou is a hybrid of African Vodun and Catholicism," replies the Morrigan. "The slaves identified with her because her mother was a Pictish slave, however if you go back even further you'll discover she's my daughter, Brigit, healing Goddess of light."

"When I was following that ship, built of Irish wood, I sensed that the forest dwelling spirits were still embedded in the walls. They talked to me, via my Mother, Goddess Danu. I think the slaves on board could hear her too.

"I hope so," I say.

"African Queens have a lot in common with Celtic Warrior Queens. WE ALL LIVE UNDER ONE SKY," says the Morrigan. "The rain that is falling on us has memory and emotion. It has probably fallen in the Americas millions of times."

"Connections run deep," I say.

"GENERATIONAL TRAUMA RUNS DEEP," replies the Morrigan.

"The Sargasso Sea unites our stories. Eels can complete their life cycles there but many of the 'displaced' have never been able to close their circles."

"Dark episodes of abduction, exploitation and environmental plunder is ALL our inheritance. We must be kind to each other and learn each other's stories so deep wounds can heal," says the Morrigan. "To Listen is to Empower."

"Eel essence is about spirit magic, watching, camouflage, endurance, travel and fluidity," she adds. "We hate borders and OWNERSHIP."

The rain has stopped and the moon is in the sky.

"Can we do a healing rain ceremony?" I ask.

The Morrigan hands me a large, glimmering, ovoid pearl.

"First you must place this around your neck."

"What is it?" I ask.

"It's an Eel Pearl," she replies. "For healing with spirit magic."

We hold hands and squelch in the bog and as we chant I receive subtle shocks, sparking my Eel Kundalini. As my power rises, the Morrigan morphs back into slippery and sinewy Eel form.

We chant to ease the suffering from generational trauma. We ask Ireland to replant its ancient forests, so the forest spirits can return home. And we chant for the victims of modern slavery. There are more people in slavery today than at any other time in history and a large percentage are trafficked women and children.

"Just one thing before I go," says the Morrigan as her fibrous tail recedes into the mud. "Eels are actually hermaphrodite for most of our lives. We are gender fluid. We are all keepers of female and male energy. I say this because I don't want people to think that Goddess-centered culture is for women only. All are welcome!"

I am The Morrigan

Kat Shaw

I am the Morrigan.
See me paint my body with sacred markings as I ready myself for war.
I will lead you into combat and pledge your victory.
Your enemies will recoil as I strike fear into their souls.
I will always fight with you and for you.
As the circle of life, I am death.
Scavenging the flesh of the fallen.
I am the Goddess of your fate.
The warrior.
The shape shifter.
The Great Queen.
I am The Morrigan.
Cross me at your peril.

How to Make a GladiatHER

Bek Paroz

Once upon a time, there was a tiny girl born to a sad queen. The king was an angry man, much put upon because he did not like to be of service to others, as good kings do – but rather he believed that all should be in service to him. Especially his wife. And once his baby daughter was born, she too became property, and his to do with as he pleased. The tiny girl became an object.

The tiny girl grew up in isolation and despair. She saw her mother fade away, present in body, but less and less active in mind as time passed. By the time she was 10, her mother was gone, and only the husk of the woman remained. She watched as her mother moved like a wraith around the castle grounds, as neglected as the gardens and the surroundings were. They ate together, pretending to be a family, but in all areas, they were merely things. Pieces for the king to move around as he desired, when he desired.

They were also vessels for his rage. When anything went wrong, and they frequently did because he really was a terrible king, the girl and her mother became his outlet for his rage. The bruises would show for days, but the trauma... the trauma lasted for years. The girl became sad, like her mother.

Within her sad heart, the girl grew a fierce longing: a longing for revenge, for freedom, for greatness, for autonomy. She named herself a secret name, *Morrigan,* and she whispered it to herself late at night, once her father had left her in peace usually passed out from overindulgence; she whispered it over and over again. The crows had called this name to her when she had hidden in the woods one day. It became a chant, an incantation, and a charm against all that her physical body and her young mind were experiencing.

She chanted this name over and over again, but she did not hear Morrigan respond.

She did not realise that the first gift of the Morrigan was subjugation, but she had learned its lesson well.

Her head was bowed, her spirit was all but broken, only the flame of revenge flickered lightly within the dungeon she had made of her heart. A cold thing of iron and ice, a fortress which no one could enter, and no one could break. She kept her secret self-imprisoned within, but she had been confined for so long, she did not know who she really was, and she had no desire to unlock her heart to find out. The king would find that last spark, and he would crush that too. She knew what it was like to be defeated, to be demoralized, to be nothing but dust beneath the feet of the oppressor.

She became cold: a thing of ice, untouchable by emotion, unmoved by violence.

She left home, unable to continue in the space she was in. She had watched her mother fade, observed the decay creeping through the surrounds, reflecting the decrepitude in the king, and she could no longer take the physical assaults on her body. She was at a crossroads and knew that she must either die or fly. She chose to fly. She became flight. And so she fled.

Pursuit followed. Dark days and dark thoughts chased her through life, haunting her sleep and changing her perception of the world around her. Everything was dark, she was the feast of carrion that the predatory scavengers of the world devoured, vulnerable flesh, unformed mind, naïve in the ways outside of the kingdom she had been imprisoned in, she was meat for wolves.

She ran, fleeing her demons, her past, her cracked mind and wounded body; she rushed from one activity to another, never ceasing to move in case something caught up with her and caused her to fail, to falter, to finally seize up in fear, never to move again. She forsook physical comfort, reveling in the deformities her childhood had inflicted upon her, flaunting them to others in the hope it would repel their interest early, diminishing herself in their eyes before they could do so to her. She made herself powerful and yet invisible. She wanted to be needed and yet not needed, so that she would never let herself or anyone else down again. She became rage. And still, her demons pursued her.

She called, chanted, summoned the Morrigan again during these times and did not hear her response.

She did not know that pursuit was the second gift of the Morrigan, but she learned it well.

She chose the darkness for herself, wallowed in it, embraced it, covering herself in the spoils of war she waged on men, on the living, on the people who would rip her soul out, if she but showed it. She still had the dungeon in place of her heart and she threw the key into a river one day on impulse, to ensure it would never be found, that she would never be broken open. She became powerful in her circles, she gave fear to others, and feasted upon their sweat. She ate their uneasiness around her for snacks in the afternoon.

She crowed in delight when she moved up in the ranks of the world, gaining more power, more prestige, while still shunning all the gloss and glitter that came with it. She embraced the darkness that she had surrounded herself with and thought that this was happiness for her kind. She did not chant for the Morrigan so much anymore, as she found that she could consume others' frailty, rather than be consumed by them. And she found it delicious. She became darkness.

She grew in power and consumed more, not realizing that she was repeating the mistakes of the past, inflicting on those around her what had been inflicted on her during her childhood. She became a monster. Her father, the king, would have been so proud, had she been in communication with him. She had not. She had cut herself off so firmly, disappearing into another world, that she no longer could even find her way back to the kingdom. And they certainly would never recognize her now.

She kept changing herself. Altering her shape and herself to fit into new worlds, now a lamb, then a wolf, she shifted into a new form to keep from being found, recognized. She refused to be locked into one way of being, allowing herself to recreate at will into someone new with each change of circumstance.

Soon she did not recognize herself. She would look into the mirror and see a creature she had created, but not know its name. She could never decide if that was satisfactory and what she wanted, so she ceased looking. And she ceased caring. She lost even the desire to feed on the fear of others. It had become tasteless and only bitterness was left for her to experience. It did not fulfill her anymore. Nothing did. It all became pointless. Worthless.

Meaningless, insignificant, and hollow. She became numb. As she allowed herself to become hollow, she faded, and she started to disappear. She stopped doing the things that kept her alive, rejecting nourishment, turning away from even the pleasures she once indulged in so completely. She rejected life and started to seek an ending. She would not call it by its name, rather she heard it call her. She became death. The Morrigan reached for her and she did not resist.

She knew now that death was the third gift of the Morrigan, and she desired to learn it fully.

She chose it, listening to the Morrigan call her name. She embraced the final darkness and let the dimness fall as it would, while she slowly, easily, and willingly slipped away from life. She heard the Morrigan call her name and answered "Yes." She became nothing and embraced it. She held on to nothing, letting go of all that she had done, her past, her future, her hopes, her fears. She looked within and without and it looked the same. Nothing has no colour, no smell, no presence, no texture, no substance; she could not tell the difference between her and the nothing she inhaled and exhaled. People moved around her but she noted nothing of their presence. She spoke of nothing, thought of nothing, and embraced nothing. She desired nothing, and it provided her everything she wished for.

Time passed; she did not know how much. She barely cared, only noting that she was still present in life, despite the embrace of death. There was a flicker, a moment of light, from deep within the dungeon where her heart used to be. The flash surprised her, and for the first time in an eternity, she felt something other than nothing. She breathed in, and received air instead of nothing, for the first time in forever. It felt like hope. She wasn't ready for that, but she also felt curiosity. She thought perhaps that was a good start for someone starting from nothing, with nothing, knowing nothing. So, she became curious.

When she investigated the flicker, she realized that there was a tiny flame, kept safe in her heart-dungeon, locked away from all that she had done and had been done to her. A little soul-flame that contained herself, before the world had gorged itself on her and she, in return, had consumed darkness. Stepping further inside this neglected part of herself, she saw what had caused the flicker, and she started to sob.

The sorrow, the pain, the despair, the feelings she had frozen out from the minute she became cold; they began to thaw. A flood of emotion flowed out of her at the sight she beheld. She truly let go of all that she had locked away and stored, the rage melting, the river becoming a deluge and she released more and more of that pent-up desolation. Inside her lonely, neglected, isolated, mistreated, and unused heart, was a diamond. A thing of beauty, of light, of strength, an exquisite and splendid diamond. All that had crushed her and beaten her down, the weight of that despair and desolation had created so much pressure on her soul, it had transformed into a diamond.

Seeing that inner transformation, she became strength. She started again and she became hope. She breathed in light and became possibility. And with all of this, she realized she was The Morrigan. A warrior. A fighter. A battle-hardened, skilled-in-the-art-of-conflict, learned scholar in the ways of overcoming and surviving.

As she embraced life, hope, possibilities, and the idea that there was a future for her, she realized that her journey had transformed her, shifted her shape from a victim to a perpetrator, to a survivor, and now she chose to become a revivor. Because in all of this, she realized she had the ability to choose.

And she named herself finally and she called all of her soul into being and revealed it to the world in all its power and magnificence, no longer ashamed for anyone to see. This was the final gift of the Morrigan.

She was the GladiatHER.

She remains so to this day.

Beyond Their Eyes
Rosanna Maria Maher

When first I faced you
Long silent drums you bade to sound
With words resounding, crackling on the air....

SHINING,
     SHINING,
         SHINING HEART

They tell you to be one way, and you laugh
They try to shut you up, yet you speak louder
They diminish your gifts, blind to your sacred throne

Flame tressed warrior
Proud edge dweller
Dark well diver

SAY.... I AM.
     SAY I AM!
         I AM. SOVEREIGN.

She's Always Been With Me

Kerry Purdy

Trigger warning for self-harm.

(*Note from author: I'd like to dedicate this essay to everyone who, throughout the years, always saw the "true me!"*)

I didn't find the Great Queen. She found me.

And now I know – she's been with me since I was a small child.

Let me start by telling this story. When I was about three or four years old, a raven got into our house. That's right, a raven got into our house. My parents were freaked. They were running in circles around the house with boxes, panicked, trying to capture the bird and get it outside.

Who was the only calm one? My three or four year old self.

"Open the window and it'll fly out," I said, matter of fact. My dad gave me a weird look, but obliged. Even at that age, I could be commanding! He opened the window – and swiftly, the bird flew out.

That was one of my first memories, the raven flying into our house. I mean, what are the odds of that happening? What are the odds of a raven flying into someone's house? It had to have simply been a strange event... or was it something more? Was that when I was "marked" by Morrigan?

As I said, I was an incredibly strong-willed, aggressive child. Even battling sensory processing disorder, which made much of life incredibly difficult for me, I was a complete alpha – even as a small girl. I was not easy for my parents or my teachers!

This changed at the age of six, when my first true abuser came onto the scene.

There was something seriously wrong with this woman. She was a sick, evil individual. Don't take my word – my parents would tell you the same thing. And she was my first grade teacher.

"Leave quietly, and nothing will go on your records," the school finally ordered her. But it was too late for me. The damage was already done. Although she traumatized the entire class – half the kids were pulled out by their parents – it just so happened that I was the one she singled out the most.

"Kerry's bad. Don't be like Kerry. Don't talk to Kerry," the class was told on a daily basis. She forced another student to write my name on the board twice – for drawing a small picture instead of a big one; she grabbed me and forcefully threw me into the corner and turned me around so that I was facing the wall. "No one wants to see you!" she screamed.

She was finally ordered to leave the school – but that strong-willed, aggressive child was gone. Gone for many years. She had become a fearful, submissive shell of what she once was. We finally ended up with a wonderful, kind lady as our teacher for the last two months of school – but she couldn't undo the damage. That alpha girl was gone.

I stayed at home for many years after that. I was home-schooled because I was too traumatized to return to public school. And I finally disassociated. I withdrew into a fantasy world in my head, involving horses – I collected model horses and in my head they were "real." In my head I lived on a "real" horse ranch – with some fantasy elements (likely owing to my other love at the time, Harry Potter) thrown in there as well. This was the world where I could feel the acceptance and understanding that I couldn't feel from the outside world. And the only time that I could leave the house was once a week, for visits to a psychologist who seemed alright at first – but as time went by, he showed his true colors.

"Have you ever heard of mental hospitals? That's where people like you end up," he told me one day.

"I'll say a prayer that God makes you normal – because it's going to take a miracle for you to come into the real world," he told me another day.

I didn't think it was possible for me to be traumatized even more – but he did it.

Fast forward about a year or so later. My parents finally found a newly opened school – that after much cajoling, I agreed to attend. This was to be my first foray back into school after my trauma. I was very fearful of it, but still agreed to give it a try. After hearing my situation, the school even agreed to let me attend for simply one hour at the end of the day for the first semester. And their hearts were in the right place. However, the school was newly opened and poorly structured. Our work was supposed to be online – half of the time the system didn't even work. Our physical "teachers" were not true "teachers," but more like classroom monitors. Few were actually licensed teachers. And most were NOT equipped at all to be in such a position. And let me tell you now, few had any backbone. And few were trained to recognize me for what I truly was – a victim of severe abuse and trauma, who wanted to please. It was obviously assumed by most that I was just a naturally timid, sweet person.

But even then, even buried deep down inside, there was the tiniest bit of that natural warrior spirit that I had always had. The child of Morrigan. And there always was.

I didn't participate in their horseback riding program, not because I was afraid to, but because that teacher back in first grade would deny me participation in fun class activities. I didn't think I deserved to join in. I would always refuse to eat during pizza parties – not because I was afraid to go into the common area where the pizza was, but because that teacher would always take my lunch away from me and force me to go hungry. I thought that I didn't deserve to eat with the rest of the class. My name became "Giggles"… because you know what they say, if you don't laugh, you'll cry.

As time went by, I also experienced severe emotional and physical abuse… this time for being a girl. That's right, being a girl. I was emotionally and verbally abused, as well as physically hit and punched by male students, for the crime of being a "sissy cowardly girl"… with staff members sitting right there, seeing and hearing it with their own eyes and ears. Nothing was done. And again, however, I thought I deserved the abuse. "I'm going to kill you. I'm going to rip out your liver in front of your parents" – with teachers sitting right there.

No one knew my true dream for when I got out of school. Ironically, this "sissy girl" wanted to join the Army or the Marines… and try to be one of the first women in a combat role. I then planned to go into the fire service once I was out.

"But I can't," I told myself. "I'm too weak. I'm too much of a sissy. I'm too much of a coward. And anyway, I don't deserve to live my dreams." So when people would ask me what I wanted to do for a career, I'd say softly… "Um… I don't know… maybe work with animals?" Why? Because I thought that's what I was expected to say.

There were, however, indeed a few trained, licensed individuals at that school who did see me for what I truly was.

"She's not what she seems to be at all. She could be very courageous and strong deep down inside," a speech teacher insisted.

I'm not going to describe my last few months at that school. Let's just say that my courageous, strong, individual was trying to come back... and let's just say that I will not go into details of what was going on, let's just say that had I had access to a gun, I WOULD have brought it to school.

I said my "last few months" because we had found a newly opened wilderness boarding school in North Carolina, which I had signed up for. And let me say, that *that* was without a doubt, one of the best experiences of my life. It's what got me to realize that I love backpacking and climbing – and I'm now today involved in wildland firefighting and search and rescue. But I digress.

Although I was starting to snap, it still wasn't obvious to most yet. I was still extremely mild and compliant – not the true me at all, but still.

Hiding in the reading corner one day, I happened to glance over, a book catching my eye. "The Hounds of the Morrigan...?" I reached out and picked it up. "About a warrior goddess... from Ireland?"

I had always known that my great-grandparents had come to the United States from Ireland as teens. And, in the past year or so, I had brought up my Irish heritage whenever I could. I made sure that people were aware of it. Why? Because I thought that if people associated me with that country, they'd think I could fight back easily... and would leave me alone because of that.

But again, I digress. Back to seeing that book. Who is Morrigan? Why do I feel as though I know her?

That was the first experience that I'd had with her in years... but she reminded me that she had always been with me. Even in the fearful "Giggles" days, I was still her Alannah.[18] I have always been a warrior, a fighter. ("She's an Indigo child!" a family friend insisted after being around me for a brief period... in the Giggles days, no less.) Timid and submissive has never been the true me at all. And I was starting to realize it.

And a year later, after leaving the school in North Carolina. I finally did snap. Hard.

I cussed out and threatened whoever I could. I lashed out violently at everyone I knew. I went goth. After a while I started cutting myself – I have pictures of my arm in bloody shreds. I began drinking heavily. And I'd sit in my car and cry for hours on end.

"Why did all this shit have to happen to me? Why did I let everyone beat me up and take advantage of me?" Flashbacks of my trauma and memories of my abuse for being a "sissy girl" ran rampant. There was no bright light in my life – this was a very, very dark time.

"You're bad! The other kids don't want to see you!"
"A girl as sissy as you doesn't deserve to live!"
"I'm weak. I'm a coward. I'm a failure... a failure..."

I still wanted to go into the Army or the Marines – and now I wanted even more to fight tooth-and-nail for a combat role. Let's look at that "sissy girl" now! But I knew, deep down inside, there's no way they would take me.

Finally, it happened. I cried out to Her. "Morrigan, if I'm meant to be here... say something," I implored one night. I was honestly almost about to throw everything in. I knew that if I didn't hear anything... my knife was sharp and ready. It would be quick.

---

18 Gaelic for "child."

But somehow being able to quiet my mind for a moment... I heard it.

A strong, yet gentle, Irish voice. "You are a warrior... and you must never let anyone tell you otherwise."

And it was very brief, but the image flashed into my head: a beautiful woman with pale skin, piercing green eyes, and long black hair, wearing a long green gown.

And I knew. This was Her. This is who was always watching over me – and had never forsaken me.

I was a warrior. That's what She said. And I was my own person – not anyone else's to kick around and abuse. I WAS AND AM A FIGHTER.

After this experience, slowly but surely, my confidence re-asserted itself. And my true, natural courage, strength, and warrior spirit finally began, after all these years, to re-emerge.

All these combinations of circumstances had held me back for all these years. My extreme trauma and abuse throughout the years – and the consequent C-PTSD and hebephrenia that resulted. My rage, my cutting, my alcoholism. My guess is, had circumstances not turned around when they did, I truly would have at least attempted suicide – or quite possibly turned to drugs. But as of last year, I was able to graduate our local community college – with my AAS in Criminal Justice, nonetheless. I hope to use it to help reform many aspects of the system, capital punishment in particular.

I didn't get to realize my true dream – to pave the way for women in combat roles. I would have LOVED to. But instead, I'm paving another path – to show what individuals can do when they're believed in and given a chance. I am now a state guard, and as I said, I'm also involved in firefighting and search and rescue. I also hope to become involved in both autism and LGBT advocacy.

And a lot of this I believe I truly owe to my experience with Her that dark night, when I had pretty much given up all hope. After that night, very little by little, my life started to turn around...

She doesn't want to be worshiped – simply honored and respected. And I stand next to Her as Her equal – not as her submissive. She appears to me as an ordinary Gaelic woman – long black hair, pale skin, green eyes. Sometimes She's dressed in Gaelic battle attire. Sometimes She's dressed in a long green or purple gown. And sometimes, She's even wearing modern street clothes!

Yes, I still have C-PTSD – and likely always will. I still do at times cut myself. And the trauma will likely never truly go away. I like to think of myself as damaged – but not broken.

"Kerry's our angel" teachers would say in the Giggles days, seeing a temporary, fleeting side of me. I am no longer an angel – I am a goddess. A Warrior Goddess, no less. Just like She who has always been there for me.

I am not just a child of Morrigan – I am an Indigo. I know the world isn't all sweetness and light. I know you've got to have a dark side to get through this world. And I say, bring it.

I still like to dress goth quite a bit. I enjoy writing dark and gothic stories and poetry. I adore darkwave and gothic metal – music that used to TERRIFY me in the Giggles days. Now it gives me comfort. I enjoy the darkness.

And there are times when I do slip up and break down. But I don't beat myself up for it. I've trusted in Morrigan – and She's made me the fierce individual I always have been. Everywhere I go, I see and hear ravens – the animal sacred to Her – and the memory of the raven somehow getting into our house when I was small will never escape me.

Lately I made a surprising discovery. The "sacred cave" of Morrigan is located in County Roscommon, Ireland... ironically not far from the birthplace of my great-grandmother!

A Pagan Prayer to the Raven
Nicola O'Hanlon

I see you in the half light
weary with pain,
I hear you screech your war cry,
Badb, Macha, Morrigan.

Sisters of Éire
hold our hearts close,
they have buried our bodies
without cross, without prayer
or the holy ghost.

Tuath Dé Danann,
your people they bleed,
revenge for their bloodshed
Our Pagan Lore decrees.

Hail wise raven,
Goddess of our Land,
may we awake in the morning
between life and death and with
power in our hands.

Sovereignty Under The Morrigan

Joey Morris

So speaks The Morrigan as I muse how to begin, to unravel the mystery of Sovereignty once again, reforging, realigning and yet never quite defining what it means to know it under Her path.

It is Shadow; the deep parts of the self, wounded and hurting, rising up in the blood as the Eclipse falls, knowing yourself when all the lights go out, and you are alone in the dark.

Listening to the whispers, discerning which are your own grinning back at you, wild, tempestuous, unfettered by the bone cracking restraints of restrictive conditioning. They can be cruel, these hidden parts of self, unhealed, called unlovable, the tendrils of the self squashed for reasons that surely made sense once upon a time.

The stories they told you, the lies, the bonds made flesh of self mutilation, a list of all the things you "are or are not" which you never sought to claim and yet remain anyway. The Morrigan snaps her raven talon fingers and they dissolve like mist over the bonfire, and all that remains is the soot-dragged remains.

"So much for their thoughts," She sneers with a bloody grin, and that's how it starts. Begin again, and again, and again, because the fire in your blood burns hotter and longer than anything that comes flailing from the outside seeking to brand you at the end of a hot poker.

My journey with The Morrigan is a constant cycle of defining and redefining what personal Sovereignty means. It is the unpicking of arrogance and privilege, neither of which are nourishing to the soul or helpful to the path.

Arrogance and privilege are instead the vehicles of oppression, weapons of weakness that are easy to hide behind when one feels wounded or attacked.

It is easy to answer with disdain, to seek out haughtiness and superiority when angered, to guard a broken heart, but what does it serve? Who does it serve? Certainly not ourselves for we seek to overpower when we feel threatened, which sounds like a futile manoeuvre, we cannot undo a wound by pretending it does not exist.

If Sovereignty is, from its roots;

> late 13c., "superior, ruler, master," from Old French *soverain* "sovereign, lord, ruler," noun use of adjective meaning "highest, supreme, chief"

... then surely we must know that the only person we can have true mastery over is ourselves.

Seeking to oppress others is a symptom of lack within.

Sovereignty can be tearing off feeling under attack and questioning which battles you actually want to show up to. What is worth your time, your energy, your peace of mind? When is it someone else's list?

I have had men calling me stupid and threatening me with rape and murder because I chose to be an ally and speak against racism. I have had people claiming I "invite" enemies or create them by choosing to speak out.

They crave my silence, my obedience. They shall never have it.

I have learned to trust when I turn my back to hatred, that there is a shield there.

The Morrigan built me from Stardust and Roots, Resilient, Proud, Hopeful. I must check myself time and again, and it is my honour to do so.

I must not fall into the trap of seeking to protect my wounds. I honour them, I wash them clean, and allow them to heal.

The chattering of the hateful falls to the wayside. The only person they will undo is themselves.

And so it is.

On the Wing of Morrigan

Barbara O' Meara

The Vigil

Arlene Bailey

They came in calling.
I could hear them from afar
as their caws grew louder
and wings in flight created a
cacophony of sound.

As they settled in the surrounding
trees, their piercing black eyes
watching my every move,
I knew they weren't here to pick the
flesh off the bones of her now dead body.
That would come later after the
soil creatures had their fill and offered
themselves to the creatures of the air.

No, they were her sentinels, here to hold
Vigil for the Sacred act of death that returns
a child of the mother back to her womb.
With silent eyes they watched as
I focused on the act of ritual.
Honoring life and death
they watched.

Three flew in and settled together
on one branch, with eyes that
pierced my very soul and a
wisdom that needed no words
to tell me who they were.

These three were the Corvids
of myth and legend.
The Morrighan in her three guises
that stoked fear in mere mortals,
but oddly brought a sense of peace
to the grief of the day.

For what seemed like an eternity our
eyes locked as I bowed to each one...
Badb... Macha... Morrigu...
as they in return acknowledged me
and the ancient magic I was working.

Three flew in to honor my beloved dead.
Hail the Traveller.

Arlene Bailey ©2020

Awaken the Morrighan

Arlene Bailey

Out of the depths of memory she rises.
From that place in the annals of myth with
eyes wide open she steps into the light.

Rooted in her own deep knowing she
embraces the sword she finds in her hands,
dripping with the blood of the Patriarchy as
Her battle cry rings with the truth of
all the atrocities laid upon women.

Crow Goddess and Warrioress,
Queen and Smith,
Shapeshifter, Fae and Poet,
Wielder of the bloody sword that
strikes for truth and sovereignty.

Awaken The Morrighan.

Arlene Bailey, ©2021

My Morrigan Story
Sam (Bo) Thompson

I'd like to tell you a little story about how I became a priest for Herself. And by Herself, I am speaking of the Great Queen, The Morrigan, The Morrigu, An Morrigan. About 25 years or so, I discovered paganism, and I began to work with Wicca, Egyptian studies, and even Hinduism, looking for the right path for me. During this time, I didn't work with any particular deity, just God and Goddess as archetypes.

But then It happened; she showed up. I remember the night well. I was relaxing on the porch enjoying an adult beverage, minding my very own business when I heard Her say, "I need you, I have work for you to do." It wasn't out loud, more of a voice in my head, and yet it wasn't. It was most certainly clear. And I knew immediately Who it was. It was The Morrigan. I did what I think most sane people would do, and laughed. I mean, full belly-almost-hysterical laugh. "No, you don't. This is NOT the droid You are looking for." I really didn't know much about Her, but I did know enough to know this was not a hill I wanted to die on, so I laughed it off and went back inside.

This could have been where the story ends, but this is The Morrigan we're talking about. She was relentless, the process of her trying to awaken me lasted for months, and nothing that I could do would make her go quiet. She pursued me with dreams and coincidences, until I had no choice but to pay attention and enter into Her service.

Which I did, jumping in head-first. I did it because I'd never had a God or Goddess pursue me. It was flattering if I'm honest, and it felt good to be wanted and needed. She didn't seem scary to me as I had imagined She would be. I had a sort of respect for her, the way you do a police officer or drill sergeant; it wasn't fear I had for her, but admiration and respect for her authority.

So, I wrote out my ritual of dedication. Now I'm an all-in kind of guy and am not known for doing things half-ass. I dedicated myself to Her; everything, forever, including priesthood (this will be an important point a little bit later). I gave myself no wiggle room. None. I didn't realize at the time that what I was doing was entering into a contract with her, with no opportunity to back out, and that I'd had the option of entering into this relationship slowly, giving myself a time limit, or an out. Hindsight being 20/20 though, I don't think I would have done anything differently.

My first task as her dedicant was to go on a mission for information. I read everything I could find. Some of the information seemed to fit what I knew and had experienced of her, other information did not. In my search, I found some people stuck mostly to the mythology and lore that was available, and this resonated with me a lot, as I liked to base my research on whatever facts were available. I took class upon class upon class; it was like drinking from a fire hose. And then, I had an opportunity to take a 6-month intensive class on Her, but I chose not to. I had a long list of excuses as to why not; my wife and I had just moved, there was work to be done on our home and property. The financial investment and my lack of higher education made me feel like the expense and the workload couldn't be justified. Oh yes, I had many excuses to give myself, though we know that since this is The Morrigan we're talking about, that I wasn't going to get out of it with a few flimsy excuses.

This does not mean that I slacked off on my studies or the deepening relationship with Her, though. During this time, I started working on my priesthood, although I didn't see it as such at the time. I'm a veteran, so I began to work with the Veterans Treatment Court, helping other veterans with substance abuse and non-violent crimes rehabilitate and get their records expunged. I became a mentor to veterans in this program as it was something that She wanted me to do.

There was a small problem, however. I often enjoyed an "adult beverage" in the evening after work. One night, one of my guys called for help from me. That night, "an event" occurred and now, I no longer drink. No one was hurt, and nothing was damaged, but it was a close call, and I knew this was Her way of showing me that alcohol wasn't something I should be ingesting anymore. I haven't had a drink since, and I still work for the Veterans Treatment Court, and this experience helped me to realize that whenever She gives me these "polite suggestions," I take the hint and listen.

Something I haven't mentioned yet, is that I'm also an amateur blacksmith. It started out as a hobby many years ago, but now it's become the way I earn my living and a way that I tap into The Morrigan and serve Her, and the community. I also offered teaching during weekend classes and showed off my skills at festivals, but then in 2020 all that came to an end with the appearance of the Coronavirus and the global pandemic. Now there were no festivals, no weekend classes, no community to serve. It was a very uncertain time for me, but The Morrigan had a plan for me. That six-month intensive course I'd tried to get out of earlier? Well, now was the time according to Her. What?! I mean, I had the time, but what about the financial burden of it? But something deep down in me told me she was right, so I made a deal with The Morrigan; if you supply the money, I told her, I'll take the course.

After several months of isolating away from other people, my craving for socialization was palpable. While my wife would be happy living on an island surrounded only by nature and animals, I need human contact. So, I started forging live through my Facebook page (Ravens Keep Forge), just for the company. It was a great way to build up my inventory, but it also gave me an opportunity to chat with other people in the community. After several months, a retailer who watched regularly placed several orders matching almost exactly what I needed to enroll in the Meeting the Mórrígan six month intensive at the Irish Pagan School. I knew this was Her hand in things, ensuring that I would not only have the money to take the course, but that I also got the potent reminder that I was here to do Her work. She wasn't going to make it easy for me, but she'd at least provide the path forward.

So, I enrolled and was accepted in the Intensive. It's been a life changing experience, and has also been a catalyst for my smithing work. Up to this point, I had only forged a few things for Her, but as I became more involved in the community, others wanted me to smith items for their altars and their practice. I have morphed into what I call a Magickal Blacksmith. I forge items within a sacred ritual space for others to help them do their work. I find the etymology of the parentage of The Morrigan very interesting. Her father's name – Delbáth – means "shaped in fire" or "fire shaper." Her mother's name – Ernmas – means "iron death" or "death by Iron." To me that screams blacksmithing. While The Morrigan isn't necessarily a goddess of smithing, I do draw similarities between the act of forging, and the processes she puts her followers through, forging them in the fire of their own experiences and shaping them into better versions of themselves.

As another part of my service to Her, I started a Morrigan study group. There seems to be so much misinformation out there that is not grounded in Her lore, but in Unverified Personal Gnosis. At the end of the Intensive, the subject of priesthood came up. At first, I was like "Nope, I'm good! Y'all go for it and I'll cheer you on!" but it kept nagging at me, and I couldn't figure out why. Until I went back and reread my dedication from years back, and there it was! Written clear as day in my own hand: Priest. Dadgummit!

One of my definitions for priest is being in service to others. I've been fulfilling that in a number of ways, including leading online rituals. It was helpful for my community and I am being in service. Being a past leader of a CUUPS chapter, I really didn't want to get back involved in the community that way as I've struggled a lot with Imposter Syndrome. My experience with The Morrigan is historically not what I would call "comfortable," and growth for me has been really hard, as I don't like to be uncomfortable or vulnerable. While forging one day I got a clear picture of myself as a ship at dock. I was comfortable, stationary, a useful object, but not being used. Then I heard Her say, "That's not what ships are for." And I knew what she wanted me to do.

Like this essay. I didn't seek this out; instead, it was brought to my attention by a friend. "You should do this" they said. But I am not a writer. I tried to get out of it. I reached out to a writer friend whom I thought would side with me, thinking that would be the end of it. But to my horror, she said, "You should do it." *Gee, thanks for nothing.* I reached out to another friend. "It must have been brought up for a reason, you should do it." *Well, you're no help.* I finally thought I had an out with the publisher themselves, as so far almost all their publications have been by women... *Nope.* So here we are.

As a devotee to The Morrigan, I make sure to include her in multiple parts of my day. Some mornings my devotions are as simple as lighting a candle. I may offer prayers with incense and water, usually lasting five to thirty minutes. I also end my day at Her altar. I am building a relationship with Her, and relationships take work. If I "run out of time" to do journey work or studying during the week, it's not uncommon for Her to wake me up around 3 AM. "How about now?" I think this amuses my beloved, Julie. "What didn't you get done?" she'll ask as I get up. *Haha – very funny.*

When I first started on this journey with Her, I thought She wanted me because of my past, with Her being a War Goddess and me being a veteran. That may be true; I don't know for sure, but I do know She wants me to be a foot.

Let me explain. Look at the modern-day army. Only about 25% are actually combat. That means roughly 75% are in a supportive role. They are all needed to make things work. Some are needed to be hands or eyes, and some are needed to be on the ground. This has been the single hardest thing for me to learn. I'm a control freak of epic proportions. I needed to have everything planned out and be in control of my own destiny. That is no longer the case. Now I just have to focus on foot stuff. Do my work, and I know She will handle the rest.

This has not been an easy path in any way, shape, or form. For me growth is hard. Change is hard. Am I better off? Absolutely! I have no regrets. I am a much better person because of Her. My personal view of The Morrigan is that she is a shapeshifter Goddess. I think She shows up how I need Her to – or how She needs me to see Her. She is a multilayered Goddess. She is hard on me, and I know she has high expectations of me. I know others view Her differently, but that is the wonderful thing about Her, she is so many things at once, and day-to-day, you never know which side of Her you'll get.

My Morrigan

Ashley McCormack

I had lost the ways of prophecy,
lost all the ways the birds speak to me,
the ways the moon makes thin places in my knowing.

This year, the battles are too many.
But the crow queen, that blessed phantom hag,
She who keeps watch at the boundaries,
has stepped out of the shadows.

She arises to meet me on every field,
beside me with every ending and beginning.
I call to her with offerings of fear,
and She honors me with valor.

With renewed strength,
I hear the geese bless this morning,
just as the full moon dallies with the daylight.

And my warrior goddess, my Morrigan,
She anoints me for the coming chaos.

Channeled
Rosanna Maria Maher

The Price of Answering her Call

Sionainn McLean

I was shaking. The bridge was wide and sturdy, but I wasn't sure what would be past it. She had led me to this moment, and I was terrified. I had created a cave for myself, just me and my family. I focused on raising my kids and put myself on hold. I never intended this to last as long as it did, but sometimes life just does weird stuff.

The past is the past, she whispered, and you are here now. Keep going.

It was 2018, and I hadn't left my home on my own in a very long time. At least not since my husband and I had kids, and maybe not before that. Sure, my husband and I traveled together now and then, but this was different... I was 200 miles from home, about to enter this camp with a bunch of people I didn't know.

I had tried to talk myself out of going. I wasn't ready, I lied. Every little bump I hit, I said that maybe it just wasn't meant to be.

The Morrigan refused to let me get out of this. Her voice was clear and loud, echoing in my head. You will not back down. You will face this, and you will overcome this challenge.

I mean, sometimes, you just don't say no—no matter how much you might think you want to. You can't, because in the deepest parts of your heart and soul, you know this is what you need to do. She knows it, which is why she's pushing you forward, inciting you to fight. Some people might not see the battle you are facing, but it's still a battle. Your battle.

My battle. I had lost myself. Don't get me wrong, I loved my husband and my children. But a long time ago, I set aside my own

142

goals and dreams so I could support my family in the best way I knew how. I began to lose bits of myself under the title of mom and wife. I felt as though I had no identity outside of those names. I couldn't remember what I wanted from life, though I knew I wanted something.

The Morrigan appeared at several points in my life, I had realized as I looked back. As a survivor of emotional, physical and sexual abuse, She gave me strength. I had endured, I was resilient, I never gave up. I might get up slower at times, but I never fully stayed down because she was in my life, whispering, pushing and urging me to keep fighting. It might've taken me a while to know her name, but I knew her.

Back at the bridge, I slowly dragged my suitcase across it, not looking back at the Uber driver who was too freaked out by the tiny bridge to drive across it. One step at a time I walked, the wheels of my suitcase thumping as they hit each board. There were people by a cabin up the road from the bridge, sitting at a picnic table.

Oh Gods, people... my heart was racing now. I couldn't turn back. I had to find my voice.

Well? I could see her smile.

When I first found the Morrigan's Call Retreat back in June of 2017, there had been that smile from her too. The event had just finished, but there would be another one the following year. Yep. That. That's what you need to do.

It was months later, and I somehow stumbled on it again, this time, with registration open. Register.

But... it's so far. And how would I get there? Can I afford it? I... don't know.

Silence, but it was the sort of silence that was an answer. She was telling me to answer this call. That I would find a way. That this was something I HAD to do. Not for her, but for myself.

I registered. I told myself that I have until April to get a refund if I changed my mind. (You are not changing your mind, she laughed.) April came, and I had to say yes or no. I still had time to cancel, to not face this. That's when the fears started rising, and she put a sword in my hand. Fight this fear. Overcome it. This is what you need. This is where you can start to heal.

I didn't cancel, even if I thought I really wanted to. A part of me worried I couldn't do it, that I couldn't leave my family behind, even for a few days, or that I couldn't face strangers. I even had a few anxiety attacks, but the whole time, The Morrigan shook her head, letting me know I could do it and that I'd be fine.

May came, and I had to arrange transportation. The family would need the car while I was gone, and it felt unfair to ask my husband to drive 3 hours to drop me off at the event, then 3 hours to return. Trains felt expensive, and it was nearly 8 hours of travel! I could just take the hit, I told myself. It's a lot of money but... a sense of disappointment washed over me. It was not my own, but it became my own. If The Morrigan believed I could do this, I could do this, right?

Right. You're beginning to understand.

When I realized I'd have to travel a day early since my situation was rather unique (there were no trains arriving before the event started!), I nervously reached out to the organizer. This was yet another silly thing that tested my resolve. The Great Queen smiled as I stepped outside of my comfort zone to make arrangements with someone I didn't know.

Walking up and speaking to these total strangers wasn't any easier. "Excuse me." My voice might've wavered a little. Maybe it squeaked, I don't know. I introduced myself, told the group of people at the picnic table why I was there, and that I had made arrangements with the organizer to arrive early. Oh gods, I thought, they are going to think I'm some weirdo...

She smiled, and there was a heavy feeling, like someone putting a hand on my shoulder. The dread and nervousness I felt slipped away as I was greeted by some of the most badass women and men I've ever met. Oh, there were to be many more trials that weekend and beyond. I faced more fears and discomfort than I care to admit: the dark, being alone in a cabin in the woods, being cold, reaching out and befriending strangers. But this was the first time I truly answered her call, I realized. I left my hermit self behind; I left my comfort and my limitations behind and answered. The introverted me found that she was capable of being outgoing when she wanted to be.

It might sound cliche to say that this was the beginning of a new life for myself, but that's exactly what happened. A new path began to form, right before my eyes. It wasn't all pleasant. I had fears to conquer, I had battles to win. I had to cut away some rotting parts of me, and it left me exposed and hurting.

Sometimes I thought I couldn't go any further. But each time, The Morrigan was there, helping me find my strength, showing me how to heal, and how to grow stronger. The Great Queen taught me that I had a voice, and she led me on a journey to find the bits of me I had lost.

Because I answered her call, I found my strength and my courage. I was able to take control of my life that I had let spin uncontrolled. I left home unsure – and returned a queen.

My Name is The Morrigan

Arna Baartz

Calling in the Morrigan

Teresa Hess

No no no no nonononononononono no! I don't want to feel like this again. This dark October feeling blowing in.

Please, please dear God, dear Goddess, please help me, don't make me go here, don't take me here again, into the dark dead feeling inside myself.

No no no no nooooooooooooo! Where is it, where is this feeling, where does it live in my body right now?

Feel in there and peel back what this is, in my face, in my head, a fog, a gray, a grieving.

Yes, grief and anger.

For what?

For all that I don't have, for all that is missing, for all that is changing, for my children grow-ing, for another year gone by, for the earth spinning, for life spinning, for the leaves falling, for the cold coming, and the dark coming, and the rain, the gray, the winter, the heaviness, the wet, dark, cold loneliness.

I am screaming into the emptiness, the void, the nothingness, the vacuum, where I am aloooooooooooooonne.

I am screaming this inner scream, or is it Her screaming, is she screaming in me?

Yes, she is here, the Phantom Queen, the Morrigan.

She enters with her raven feather cloak, her dead leaves, her smoke and gray, her cold, wet and darkness.

She sits on my chest forcing me to notice her.

Takes my face in her hands and makes me stare into her eyes and she reminds me, she says,

> "Here too, this is a part of life. This death, this grieving, this giving up, this letting go, this crumbling, this destruction.
>
> This is the other side of the coin, the coin you covet, but you only want to look at the bright side, the shiny side, the alive and sunny blossoming side but you
>
> YOU
>
> are also the dying side—always being re-born, yes—but always dying.
>
> Make love to the Void. Dance with me."

This Morrigan, is another kind of Lover. She is wise and deep, she is frightening and powerful.

She will scream through you, as she is screaming through me. She is a crone, a shapeshifter, a magician, a dark goddess, a warrior, a reaper.

She is Nature. She is Change. She is Death. She is Wild. She isn't clean or pretty or predictable.

She isn't happy. She isn't Joy. She isn't soft and nurturing. Her nurturing is brutal.

Screaming, crying, howling, destroying---
Lose it all to her! With her dark kiss and penetrating glare.

She will call you into your wider, deeper self over and over again in the most crass and honest, howling ways.

You will wail. You will be stripped. This will all be taken away from you.

All of it!

You will be barren, empty. You will be naked and decayed, destroyed, a pile of bones, and then nothing.

She will howl through like the wind and blow you and all you know away, and you must bow to her and thank her and make her offerings of gratitude.

For without her, nothing comes about. Without her, there is no change, no growth, no evolution.

Without her, the shells won't crack. The seeds won't grow.

Without destruction there is no creation and there is no creation without her destruction.

She is wind, she is fire, she is storm, she is death, she is out of your control.

Can you dance with her? Can you let her in?

Can you kiss her? And be consumed by her and feed off her wisdom?

She is screaming for you to look at her, acknowledge her, be whole by uniting with her too, with your own emptiness, with your own grief.

Howl, shrivel, turn to ash, vacate, die—so that you may truly Live.

With the wisdom and the knowing and the depth and the darkness and the wholeness the Dark Goddess brings.

Call in the Morrigan. Dance with Her. Surrender.

Darkarma

Sharon Smith

Blind me,
crack my ribs,
break my leg...

I came to you with pure Love,
but that wasn't good enough, was it?

You tossed me aside,
threw me under the bus
and watched it roll over me.

Then you walked away,
never looking back.

FYI:
Sorry, it didn't kill me.

What's that old saying?
"What doesn't kill you makes you stronger."

I survived.

I rose up,
bent-legged,
one-eyed,
ache in my side, where my heart
once beat for you...

I rose up
Stronger.

Angrier.

And I'm coming for you.

When I find you,
"A woman scorned" will seem
a hollow, empty threat,
for my wrath will be so much greater,
my fury worse than a raging wildfire.

But like that wildfire,
I
Will
Burn
You.

Oh, yes
I will devour you till there is nothing left
but a memory.

And like a spark in the wind,
that too shall quickly fade.
And you will dwell in utter Darkness,
in the Unknowing forevermore.

Oh...
Did I forget to tell you, that is my Home?
Too late!
Welcome to your eternity...

[Author's Note: This is a Dark Goddess take on the theme of "A Woman Scorned", a modern interpretation of The Morrigan's story]

Morrigan II

Laura Cameron

The Raven and the Wren

Erika Lopp

Once Upon a Time, long ago, in a time before remembering lived a great king and his nine children, five daughters, and four sons, each inherently magical and blessed with a special gift.

So the tale goes that the nine "Powers" as many came to call them spread out to the farthest reaches of the earth. There they used their special gifts to help and heal the land.

Now the King's eldest daughter was the powerful Queen Morgana Le Fey, who the Irish people knew as both kind and just. Morgana, who possessed many talents, used her gifts to aid the dead in their passage to the other worlds. As time passed Morgana became associated with both death and war, often being seen by the dying on the battlefields. At times, Morgana would heal the fallen soldiers, for the Queen was skilled in the arts of healing herbs and enchantment. The Raven became her totem, the bird perched upon her shoulder as she walked the fields at night in search of lost souls.

In time, Morgana's image turned from friendly and kind Queen, who aided the people in times of dreaded warfare, to both dark and terrifying Goddess. Though this representation couldn't be further from the truth, this archetype prevailed.

Morgana cried out to her father in despair, "Why do they judge me?"

"Is the moon not as beautiful as the sun?" "Is the moth not as important as the butterfly?"

"Is the darkness to be feared?"

Often Morgana would sit with her father high on the Irish mountaintops overseeing their many kingdoms. Here her father imparted to her this great wisdom.

"The people fear death, thus see it as a loathsome, a horrible state. They do not realize death is but a beginning, a passage to yet another life. *Hence they see You as a representation of death.* They fear you, for they do not see you for what you truly are."

"My daughter, you are a powerful force of renewal on this land. You are not death, but rebirth, not darkness, but a gatekeeper who lights the way to the other worlds."

"Morgana, you are the weaver of shadows, the one who invokes change in the hearts of all she touches."

"The people's fear of death is great, thus they fight us and each other, in doing so they perpetuate great evils upon the land in the forms of war, judgement, and discord."

"I weep for them and hope that the truth may one day be understood. That death is not to be feared but celebrated, as the people of old once knew."

Reassured by her father's wisdom, Morgana continued her earthly mission as healer to the fallen, protectress of the people, and guide to those in transition between life and death.

Years spun by and Morgana's notoriety faded with the passage of time.

But for those who do recall her, she is still viewed as a dark and destructive force. Sadly, the Misunderstood Queen still cries out,

"Is the Raven not as lovely as the Wren?"

The Young Sovereign

Andrea Redmond

Mysteries of the Dark

Kay Turner

I am Priestess of the Mysteries of the Dark.

I walk with you into and through your shadow lands offering you a cloak of protection for the journey.

I retrieve your blazing heart from the entombment of despair, pain and shame.

I am Holy hell raiser.

I am the one who watches and waits whilst you put on the armour of procrastination, bypassing, denial, gossip, projection, competition, neglect and criticism until you realise it's too heavy to wear.

I am protector of your maiden, mentor of your mother, fuel of your lover and trainer of your huntress.

I am hermit and oracle, lone wolf and guide of the pack.

I am receiver and transmitter, reflective and invisible.

I have no interest in small talk. I am she who sees. I am she who places the mirror in front of you until you see your truth and power. And own them. Fully. And it embodies them. Fully.

I am Mistress of the Goddess. The embodied expression of the gift of new beginnings through living death.

Photo by Kay Turner

Sword at my Back

Karen Storminger

Iridescent darkness envelopes me
Glossy, black, wings
My shield against the onslaught of the world
My hand reaches behind me
My palm caresses the hilt of my Sword
Forged from all the hurt, pain, fear and anger
A lifetime's worth
Stored deep within my marrow
Transformed into a formidable weapon
Cradled in its sheath, my spine
Calm descends
An opening appears
My time has come
Your smile reaches my lips
The enemy falters
With unsheathed fury
I claim what is rightfully mine

Strength in Softening

Jessica Johnson

With the rise of women-positive movements, marches and protests these days, I think the concept of women being strong has been almost done to death. Proof that women are strong is everywhere, from the rise of women seeking to deliver their babies medication-free or at home, Instagram-superstar yogi women who can balance on their hands; Pussy Hat march movements; and the women taking the stand in public to recount their sexual abuse despite thousands of people accusing her of lying or attention-seeking. The spotlight on the strength of women is more powerful than ever before, and the pressure to keep going is real. But with all of this emphasis on strength, I think that we as women have forgotten how important softening and being compassionate can be.

When I first began working with The Morrigan I thought that most of my journey would require me to endure difficult, emotional lessons, and that I'd need to be perpetually armed to the teeth to fight for social justice for women and the pagan community. And my journey with her has definitely required me to be strong, and I've felt like I was being jerked around emotionally a few times too. But by and large my biggest takeaway from The Morrigan is the importance of softening towards the big, hard feelings like grief, unworthiness, self-loathing, anger, and sadness. I used to think that when the big black waves of sweeping emotions came my way that I needed to harden my heart, turn a blind eye to them, and ride out the storm. But trying to rise above all those feelings was not working for me anymore, and when I asked The Morrigan for advice on how to tackle these big emotions, she told me to soften, to open myself up to them, and let them in.

161

My first response, obviously, when I was asked to completely open myself up to the pain of the death of a loved one, or the highs and lows of depression and anxiety, was fear and repulsion. I had prided myself on being "strong" before, so strong that I didn't need to really experience these emotions anymore, but rise above them. I wanted so badly to emit this Buddha-like zen whenever something catastrophic happened to me, but instead of rising above the water like a lily I felt more like I was drowning in the mud at the bottom. And every time I heard The Morrigan say "soften" I gave in to my fear and I scrambled as quickly as possible to toughen up, determined that this time I would rise above the heart ache like the mental master I supposed myself to be. Time and time again I floundered, and wondered why my matron was putting me through this constant battle with myself, why she kept sending me wave after wave of emotions and why it felt like she never bothered to save me from near-drowning in them.

Eventually, I stopped ignoring her and took her advice. Trusting that I would survive was one of the hardest things I've had to do during my adult life, it was painful, it was overwhelming, and it was… glorious. I opened my heart up to feeling everything that came my way in a way that I likened to opening all my doors and windows to the weather in the middle of a hurricane. I was immediately buffeted by immense, over-powering feelings of guilt, anger, shame, self-loathing, insignificance, depression, nervousness and fear, but the longer that I stood in the torrent of those emotions, the more I felt their power to connect me with other people, all experiencing the same things. Escaping these emotions wasn't going to make me more mature, more spiritual, or get me closer to the divine, it was cutting me off from them!

The power of really knowing how someone feels when they open up to you is a gift, the gift of empathy, the gift of survival, the gift of being able to look someone in the eyes, see their pain, and really connect over a shared experience of that emotion. And it doesn't just go for the traditionally "negative" emotions like grief or suffering either, it's also true with pleasure, happiness, contentment, joy, and belonging.

I never thought that while working with The Morrigan that I would find myself in the position of learning how to take *off* my armour, but here I am, a very introverted person, a woman who identifies as an empath and intuitive, and someone who has dealt with depression and anxiety since I was in my mid-teens. I've survived a suicide attempt, an abusive marriage, bearing two children into this world, the betrayal of best friends, abandonment by family members, several deaths of family and friends in the last ten years, and the trials that come with being a woman in today's western world, and one that self-identifies as a witch at that. I have born all the typical hallmarks of someone who should be closing myself off to the pain of the world like sexual abuse, mistreatment in the workplace, renovating my home (okay, so that's being a little big melodramatic, but seriously, if you want to test your relationship, do a home reno together...) divorce, and so much more. Instead of calcifying a tough shell around me though, I've learned to soften in response to these emotions, to take the lessons they have to teach me into the very DNA of my cells, and reprogram my responses to them of grim determination to take as much of the lesson into me as possible, instead of trying to just survive them. I look for the opportunities to grow, rather than ways to get through it quickly and painlessly, and to me, this is the mark of a true warrior.

Don't think that softening has lessened my resolve to uphold healthy boundaries though! Oh no! I may be able to open myself up to empathy and compassion more quickly and easily than before, and to reap more of the lessons from a bout of depression or anxiety, but it doesn't mean that I'm willing to let people walk all over me or use me. The true path of a spiritual warrior, I feel, is a balance of strength and softness. They are two sides of the same coin, and each are valuable in a personal spiritual practice, as well as group settings too. You can host a Red Tent and open your circle up to women and girls of all ages and personalities, but that doesn't mean that you will accept harassment, abuse, or domineering behaviors from any of them either. The same needs to be true of how we conduct ourselves in the world, tell our stories to people who will listen, be a beacon of love when all else around you feels like it's devoid of it, but knowing when to leave before you are zapped of your own strength and are left empty and burnt out.

So daughters of The Morrigan, Hecate, Cerridwen, Modron, Kali, Hel, and more... Remember please—your strength is not always measured in how tough you are, but also in your softness, your vulnerability, and the true range of emotions that you have felt and experienced through the journey of your life. Wisdom is knowing that the sword is not always the solution—sometimes it's a hug, a knowing glance, a companionable silence, or a gentle acceptance of the circumstances.

A Reckoning with The Morrigan

Iris Eve

what arrogance you show
strutting around
like you own this place

wearing your inhumanity
like a badge of honor

you desecrate the very air
with the stench of your entitlement

your violence reeks of weakness

you feed on fear
& harness power through pain

you prey like a monster

& i have been here
silently watching you
all
this
time

i watched you violate Her daughters
i watched you enslave Her sons
i watched you poison the very well
from which you drink

you betray your own heart
you make weak your own will

& now
in Her name
i have come
wearing her wrath
bearing your fate
bringing victory to victims
i feed on monsters

i have been sent to reclaim you
devour you
decay you
turn you over
like compost
until you are humus

only then you will know humility
only there you will remember sovereignty

this is your reckoning

Mór Ríoghain – A Corvid Vision

Iyana Rashil

I began my relationship with the *Mór Ríoghain* by invoking her in an Irish tongue as Mór Ríoghain[19] to hopefully discover for myself what relationships I can have with her aside from the modern versions of lore, language and backfill perspectives that are offered. I am particular about words and where they come from as well as my invocations and what they materialize. This is because whenever I invoke a feminine otherworld being or Goddess, I ask her to reveal things beyond what is written. My experience with *Mór Ríoghain* is no different. Before I share that story, I offer a short section of a longer poem to her honor.

> *Mór Ríoghain* dressed in black wings or shields of patina green,
> Deserves honor as a Great Irish Queen
> To reign with valor, bravery and beauty
> In her heart's destiny and duty
> To show sister seekers the meaning of her ways
> How they evolve with the years and the days.
> Over and over, she speaks the way of victory,
> This time for sisters worldwide to see.
> Words are the swords.
> See this war and the new shall be born.
> Hailing the name
> The Great Queen Mór Ríoghain.

I met *Mór Ríoghain* for the first time when I invoked our initial relationship but had a more detailed experience down the road that I'd like to share here. I needed assistance from *Mór Ríoghain* as *Badhbh* (crow)[20] for visiting the dawn of queens. It was the right

---

19 www.behindthename.com, entry, Mór Ríoghain
20 www.mythopedia.com, entry, Badb

request because this is when I received my call from *Mór Ríoghain*.

I needed *Mór Ríoghain* as *Badhbh* crow to take me across time and place. She honored my request and took me on the ritual journey. We arrived on a cliff high above a mountainside forest. We sat for a moment to enjoy the vista. She eventually flew down to the forest below to an opening in the trees, a straight path was before us that seemed to go on for endless miles. We waited again. After a time, I began seeing the faces of women, one at a time, framed by the endless row of trees. Their faces were as large as the trees themselves and they kept coming toward me one after another, changing in looks and races, slowly then rapidly. I realized I was going back in time, into the forest's memories. The faces were not shown as ages as there was no accompanying apparel, but I knew they were sisters from time outside of time. Sister after sister came into my view. Eventually they shifted from happy faces to more angry until I reached the First Queens. They were enraged beyond belief. When I grew frightened and curled up under *Badhbh's* wings, they explained that they were angry because they were buried deep beneath the lies, silenced and that those lies grew heavier and heavier on top of them through time. They revealed that there was no way they could arise, except through the living sisters of the future times. As I listened, a heavy weight came upon me and grew in pressure. I could feel their burden and their longing. They were letting me feel what they felt. They continued to tell me that the sisters closer to modern times were happier because they didn't know the weight that the First Queens feel, that they had all been given crumbs of liberation through the ages as a way of foolery and deception. The First Queens spoke of the trap of the Dark Age mind as they have seen it all but could not warn of the language ploys and the trick of the crumbs of liberation.

Mór Ríoghain as *Badhbh* then revealed that this was the call of the war against the lies placed on words which placed spells on the minds of all people, especially sisters, and the crumbs which deceive. She asked if I would step up to the challenge. I accepted.

As we turned to leave, I saw crumbs all over the ground. *Mór Ríoghain* as *Badhbh* wouldn't nibble on the crumbs thrown at a million sisters' feet and flew upward instead, struggling to rise up out of the weight of time. She eventually succeeded in pulling me out as my traveling body hung onto one tiny crow foot with one hand, feeling heavy, struggling to rise, but rise we did and the message was clear. The First Queens were calling sisters to 'see' the war of freeing our sister queen selves out of a lie so intense it is like a heavy trap. *Mór Ríoghain* as *Badhbh* took me to the truth that the power of sisters is constantly being defeated by language and crumbs which pretend to be liberations, small deceptions and detours at every turn, virtually unnoticeable. *Mór Ríoghain* revealed that even her own story and truth has been tangled and mangled.

I left the First Queens that day with a *Mór Ríoghain* call with new internal knowing and a call to battle the lie as many of you may have also received. After returning and over time, *Mór Ríoghain* showed me a new way to fight the battle of words for victory. My specific call was about evolving words, breaking any spells, noticing crumbs which were deceptive. I reflected in retrospect for a moment on 'what crow doesn't like breadcrumbs'? *Mór Ríoghain* as *Badhbh* said, no more shall I eat of the lie. As *Badhbh* I am more akin to hanging with wolf packs (sister packs) for true nutrition – the magic of our natural sister ways. This birthed my first word evolution. I saw *Badhbh* corvid as a bringer of 'core vision' (a word play with Corvid as Core Vid, Core Vision, a *Mór Ríoghain, Badhbh* Crow Vision). I saw Core Vision as a 'resister of crumbs' and a 'resister of lies,' as a re-sister-ing movement—not a war but a call to becoming the new sisters rising—for all sisters as the new core seeing sisters, the corvid seeing queens. From there, I went on a mission to dig deep into any old information on *Mór Ríoghain* that I could find.

As mentioned earlier, my search began with *Mór Ríoghain's* name. In Mór Ríoghain's Irish name, she is hiding an ideal of a "Great Queen[21]" rather than some dark phantom perspective of the Dark Age language maker. Many of you have discovered this already. Moving in deeper, this was another breaking of the language spell for me, seeing the Great Queen within differently than war and omens, even though I was called to a new type of battle. This small shift made me seek deeper into the deception of the language which we know today as English, born during a dark age.

The English language records Morrigan's associations as war, death and crow, even a phantom queen. I took an etymological journey into the word 'war' and found that if you were to use original words, you might discover *Mór Ríoghain* to be a 'beautiful mighty queen of valor who was a champion heroine with drive.' Can you see how small shifts in word usage give you power and how heavy and dark the Dark Age words are?

The English word 'war' is dated middle 12th century whereas the dates for Irish counterparts are often much earlier. It is rare for English words to come from Irish Gaelic or other similar languages, so I wondered how she is related to modern war when that word wasn't even used in her part of the world yet.[22] Nor is the word 'battle' existent until the 13th century. The words war and battle are English interpretations according to a language developed using Dark Age perspective of the words borrowed from German and Old English,[23] not Irish. The English language makers have a way of thinking that they know better than any 'other' culture, but that is another story entirely.

If the original meaning of the word 'war' was to 'confuse and perplex,' or 'difficulty or dispute,'[24] then really, the word war has

---

21 www.behindthename.com, entry, Mór Ríoghain
22 Google search translations, war and warrior in Irish
23 www.etymonline.com, entry, war and battle origin dates
24 Ibid, entry, war as confusion

nothing to do with our beautiful and mighty queen. These words of war – to confuse and perplex – are still attacking today through English words. There is actually a word-war which is happening through words of the English language through a lingering Dark Age agenda (a gender).

The English word makers who spell cast as definers (deafeners) of our Great Queen turned his own delusion on her, calling her 'a fearful crone who sowed fear and confusion on the battlefield'[25] when it was more than likely he who was confused and perplexed not only on the battlefield but also about feminine powers. He blamed everything on feminine sorcery, ignoring that this was a projection of his own dark magic in word making and spell casting (spelling) and religious demonology. Even the word 'phantom,' in its root meaning is 'to bring to light; to shine.' In today's world we do not see that meaning. It is buried. It is only in the later 13th century English a phantom became something to fear.[26] This fear was in men who didn't understand the mysteries of the sisters and still don't. If he cannot understand it, he condemns it. Here is how the trickery is committed and a sister's power is taken away. Dark age language makers projected their own faults upon others. It was easier for him to say a crone confused him than to admit that he failed on the battlefield. Language is from his perspective, 'his sight' not *Mór Ríoghain* as *Badhbh* corvid core vision sister sight.

Another oddity I found about 'war' was that the word 'war' at one point in Latin was said to be derived from *bellum* and connected to 'beautiful' and *duellum* 'quite brave' and 'actions of valor.'[27] This revealed another act of deception. The dark age man took beauty and valor and turned it into war as acts of violence. This set a very different stage for me and my relationship with the now Great Queen of Valor and Beauty and her regal black feathered body as crow, able to help me see with core vision a beautiful mighty

25 www.mythopedia.com, entry, Badb
26 www.etymonline.com, entry, phantom
27 Ibid, entry, war as beauty

queen of valor who was a champion heroine with drive. In a Great Queen of Valor and Beauty, there was nothing terrible, dark or vile, just greatness which is how I came to know her. So many things today are reversed via language *deafenings*, such as how sisters know that 'darkness' represents the womb of life, not evil.

I met a Great Queen Revealer who told me how to be victorious with beauty and valor even when I call it a battle. Because 'valor' means courage doesn't mean she was fighting like Dark Age men or causing intentional confusion. In my experience she brings clarity about lies. This new aim was a call to uncover the lords of confusion.

It is not that men are bad.
The dark ages men are long dead,
but their language survives
Clouding our sister corvid core eyes.
They saw with male dark age perspectives.
That should be long gone, no longer projected.
Mór Ríoghain said, look at the world with core (corvid) sister eyes
and see the dark ages disguised and still alive
in language.

Mór Ríoghain revealed to me that with corvid (core vision), sisters could break the word spells. As I continued on with *Mór Ríoghain* as crow and crow as core vision, I saw more and more of the word spells that needed breaking. My core eyes were opened. My queen power is not violent. It is not even in a war in the sense of an English defined war. The victory is in clarifying the beauty buried beneath language deceptions in the English language 'definitions' otherwise seen as 'the *deafenings*'.

Taking words they pushed into our being into a new sister seeing.

Today the darkness becomes a womb
That place of hidden sister truth

172

A great light is there, called true sight.
This is the new war, rarely seen before
Filling in the death language with sister life.

Mór Ríoghain's, Badhbh led journey to the First Queens revealed that Dark Age English word maker projections created the language. The word spells came from his projections, his barbaric castings (his sights) which were filled with death and killing intentions, fear and superstitions, trickery and deception because that was his perspective and intention. When he looked at the world and defined it, he saw through a barbaric fear to survive and his inability to understand a sister's magic and how – when a sister looks through her core corvid eyes – she sees LIFE. If he would only seek a sister's counsel.

The balancing of the current imbalance is through sisters breaking the spells on the Dark Age language with Valor, with Beauty, with Joy and with *Mór Ríoghain* and *Badhbh* Core Corvid Vision to lift the weight of language lies. Every sister of now and then depends on this. This call seeks more than one sister. If you hear it, this is a task of sister unity. Seeking in the womb of words to find buried sister empowerment rather than believing the dark age language of confusion made by dark age men who were superstitious, concerning all feminine experiences is the aim. Sisters can restore life and step out of a deceptive language – through Mór Ríoghain, Badhbh Corvid Vision 'core vision' the pure space where the silence speaks, safe from the confusions of external language.

The victory over the Dark Age language confusion is our sister victory. For me, my sister sight concerning the word spells on language is a *Mór Ríoghain* united sister queen of valor and beauty victory. War and death were the Dark Age ways of seeing and did not represent her valor and beauty, her heroism and power. She also transitioned my ideas of sisterhood and triune consciousness in this calling. All three *Mór Ríoghain* sister representatives speak here: *Badb*, Crow, *Makaja* as the Sun of

Womanfolk and *Anu*, The Paps of Anu,[28] as Core Vision, Clarity and Nutrition from the Mother Queens of all time.

---

28 www.wikipedia.com, entries Morrigan, Badb, Makaja, Anu

I Inherit Your Name, Morrigan

Mary Ellen Talley

oh, shapeshifter / crow shadow against
full moon / death / oh, slumbering waking /
what is there about distortion / chiaroscuro
smudging / that prepares us to wear
long-forgotten garments / how can / she
be both for death and life / her rough wool /
layers of flowing silk / don't goddesses
have to choose / is she not temptress
of contradictions / fertility / combines
with fog / the crow is hiding in the dense black /
but forgets about silence / I know the crone
is coming back to trick me / compassion
is not her bailiwick / her silence harsh
ink dark / if true her breasts form hills
of Kerry / and she is bird / then mountains
fly upon the breeze / her silver beak /
her lips / my conscience conscientious
disavows her blame / my sins are plenty /
I want her story to bequeath / healing /
if I spell her name and drop / r-i- g/ dead
in the middle / I see my maiden name /
she is goddess of our family anger /
we are three sisters / cacophony
of outrage at our stumbling / though
her sisters' trinity begot St. Patrick's
that we adopted / I cannot refuse
to juxtapose this goddess /
of my contradictions / request
that she remain with me / one night /
as if upon the fog's low layer / she
might wander off / retrieve my mother /
father / sister /brother / through

a corridor of messages / of which
the sun is seeking / past / before
laurel / hawthorn / lilac bloom /she
retreats into her shrine / this passage tomb
Newgrange / where I find / my name/
my sisters' names / upon her lips

Becoming Morrigan

Barbara O' Meara

My Final Offering
Raya Elyse Bencivenga

Let it be known that when I die I want my body to be picked apart by crows.

I want to exit this earth chapter as a magnificent stinking feast, as meaty sustenance for my feathered friends.

I want them to make nests with the tendrils of my hair and rear their young off my fat backside.

I want them to fly my bones up high to drop them shattering onto pavement so that they may enjoy the soft marrow within.

True to life, I'll be as hot a mess in death as I was alive.

Honest and well-meaning despite whatever outcome awaits me.

I want my death to provide nourishment for other life.

And as I exit, I'll be grabbing pieces of this dying paradigm to take with me into the obliterating void.

Ashes to ashes, Mess to mess.

From Go to Goddess

Alyssa Spungen

It has taken me a long time to be able to bridge the ideas of the "Morrigan" and the "Goddess." The Morrigan introduced herself to me as a seed in 2015. We then became acquainted in a nighttime vision in 2016. Unpacking her story, doing my research and experimenting in different ways of connecting to Her took some time. Now, I can't differentiate the two. The Goddess is everything and the Morrigan are her flavors. There are so many delicious ones.

When I was invited by a Celtic priest to train with him as a priestess, I didn't know what the word Goddess meant, let alone what priestess meant. I only knew that I was not relating to all of the teachings that had previously been made available to me. And that nothing was going to stop me from following my gut.

He had me at "Erotic Arts of the Goddess." Is there anything juicier than that? I know it probably sounds crazy to you, that I would meet a Celtic priest online that lives in Canada, talk to him virtually for 2 years and then sell everything to buy a one-way ticket to his island. But to get an idea, I was working at a local café run by an eco-village community with a reputation of being a cult but with beautiful, locally sourced produce. I was there because I could feel something special in the air, was curious, and excited about living on my own for the first time ever. I was 24 and had just left my first live-in boyfriend's studio apartment for my own one-bedroom apartment. We broke up and within a few hours, I was having marathon sex with my neighbor Juanito which lasted about 12 hours.

He dubbed me "The Lizard Queen" and I was fucked psychic for a week. I knew when someone was about to call. I knew what people were going to say before they said it. I felt like I'd been

179

fucked out of this dimension. And you know who couldn't meet me there? The spiritual community I worked for. So, I fled for the tiny island of Erotic Arts with the Priest. I toyed with telling people, which 99.9 percent of the time induced panic in those around me and inspired me to start explaining to folks that I'm going on a Yoga retreat. Only one person was truly excited for me. Being someone who spent most of her life getting off on the things that shocked others, I was flying high, literally, when the panic set in. I was on the plane on my way to Vancouver and I started trembling. What was I getting myself into?

Luckily, Canada has really strong beer, the people are friendly and the public transit system is accessible.

The priest was perfectly friendly and accommodating when I arrived and thereafter for the next 3 years, which was how long I went into and out of the country to stay with him for my studies. Coming from the cultural background that I do, our relationship has been quite hard to integrate, despite the fact that I had struggled so hard to free myself from the dominant cultural narrative.

My time with the priest was well spent, in retrospect. During the first 3 months, I was grieving and in a state of anxiety nearly the whole time. I felt value-less, and lazy and just plain wrong, as I was not being productive for the first time in my life, or rather, not productive in the way I was used to proving, making money or getting good grades; namely, having external tokens of value. For the first time in my life, I was being productive doing whatever the hell I wanted, and it just so happened that what I wanted was to connect to my sacred femininity. The priest showed me the relationship between desire and manifestation by teaching me about rituals, circles, worshipping the Goddess, rules of magic, connecting with the elements, shape-shifting, love-making, freedom and abundance, Tarot cards, Astrology and accepting all parts of ourselves as reflections of a Divine nature. We are all of us material to be shaped.

He entitled his work, "The Civilizing Art of the Goddess" and explained that he had de-coded A.E. Waite's "Pictorial Key to the Tarot" and discovered a particular formation of the Kabbalistic World, "Br'iah," the Divine Feminine. The formation itself is a puzzle and can be deciphered in order to reflect a process of transformation that can be traced through evidence we have of the Mystical Arts reaching back to Antiquity. He helped me connect to my own ancestral roots of Judaism and invited me to become an initiate of his Celtic family tradition, which I hold with great honor.

Trying to integrate my mystical studies, practices, and shifting belief systems back into the world I had come from, was, and is a challenge. He would tell me people like us are outcasts. He made me feel more connected than I'd ever felt to another human being. He was my mother and father and lover and magician and boy and monster and friend and teacher and student all in one. Sometimes I loved him, sometimes I hated him and sometimes I was afraid of him. But he was dependable, and unattached. He showed me nature's pacing and that I'm a part of that. We laughed together, partied together, hung out together, read together, smoked together, sat on the beach together. We spent time apart too. He was an outcast on this tiny island, but a friend among those who loved him, which happened to be the coolest people there. We went on walks together. Sometimes I treated him to lunch and breakfast. We hitch-hiked. We heated up the cabin and performed lunar rituals. We watched a lot of "The Blacklist" and ate endless pieces of toast and drank endless cups of black tea. Living on that island taught me how to be a good community member.

I was consecrated as a Priestess of the Goddess without really knowing how to even talk about what that meant. I received 'swords' cards in almost all of my Tarot readings for years. I was thinking so much and had only just begun my journey to feel, another casualty of white supremacist culture, that it was difficult to understand how that *feeling,* in and of itself, can catalyze transformational shifts. He called me a "baby Dragon" which was a lineage term for a novice initiate. I felt exalted.

The times I came back to the U.S. in between visits, I had to figure out how to save up enough money to go again and stay longer. The first time, I waitressed. The second and third time? I became what it is called a professional Sugar Baby. For me, this wasn't a difficult transition due to what I had been learning and experiencing. To be "owned" by anyone, or to have to fit myself into somebody else's definition of how a 'girlfriend' or 'woman' is supposed to behave was not something I took kindly to. Not that being in a close consensual relationship with another is necessarily sacrificing our Selves, but that making those commitments before fully knowing one's Self can turn us into sacrificial lambs. All that to say, celebrating and expressing my sexuality was something I definitely wanted to practice, intentionally, and for the first time. I felt liberated by knowing more about what was inside of me, and deeper ways of feeling into my truth without having to leave my body behind in heavy intellectual pursuits.

After leaving the island, I moved back to the desert and found a group of women to be in circle and ceremony with, to connect with one another when the moon was full or new. At this point, I had only heard the name "The Morrigan" in a passive mention of the Priest discussing the reason some priestesses will serve a particular Goddess as opposed to the general Goddess. He referenced a student of his that was a priestess of the Morrigan. I remember feeling intimidated, the Warrior and Death Goddess? I thought. Wow. But the thought and the feeling were fleeting.

A couple of months after moving back to the Desert in 2016, I had the vision:

I am standing at the threshold of the front door of a large house looking out at the woods and a pathway. I was aware that one moment before I had been upset that my washer-woman had died with a load of my laundry and begged for her to come back. As I looked out at the daytime scene, more figures appeared. My friend Missy was outside by the bonfire pit, there to greet a maiden corpse in white carrying a load of white linen, perfectly folded, and walking down the dirt pathway. I was afraid to look Her in the eye but she looked at me, and I couldn't help myself. The space between us collapsed. She gave me chocolate and showed me offering it to another witch, who spit it out. I gobbled mine up. Then, she took me to the underground, which was occupied by various rooms filled with antiques. In one of the rooms, she showed me a photo album and it had me at the center of the photo, with others by my side. My face was blurred out. "Before you embrace Death," she whispered. And then she showed me another album. I was poised, confident, powerful. My eye contact was secure. "After you embrace Death." I woke up chanting "Morgannah, Morgannah, Morgannah." Like the chocolate, I gobbled up this new need to find out who She was and what Her message meant.

After that visit from the War and Death Goddess herself, I dedicated all my menstrual blood to her. It felt intense, and I also had no idea what I was doing. 'Embrace Death' is obviously a rather scary message if you take it literally. Luckily for me, The Celts did not have such a narrow view of Death that we in the United States and under white supremacist culture have. Having studied Tarot symbolism and having had a few years of living with a Druid under my belt, it became clear to me that Morgannah's message was not about my death, or that of someone I knew. As the Myth goes, Badb as the Washer at the Ford, would visit in her aspect as the Crone and be seen washing the bloody clothes of someone who was going to die in battle. The fact that she appeared to me as a maiden and with clean clothes assured me it was a message of rebirth, and it also gave me a glimpse of the shape-shifting nature of the Morrigan.

Combining my knowledge of the "Civilizing Arts" and being a Priestess of War and Death, to me, initially meant that it was my mission to find the shitty men out there and to rehabilitate them. And that I tried. It only left me feeling crummy and scared. As I ventured into new relationships, jobs, ways of being in the world, I learned that it takes a lot of pendulation and trial-and-error to find balance and to know when to show yourself and when to be invisible, know when to act and when to stay still, when to fight and when to take a step back.

After my attempts at rehabilitating men, I took some time off, gave my blood to the plants or threw it away. But my bible, Stephanie Woodfield's "Celtic Lore & Spellcraft of the Dark Goddess: Invoking the Morrigan" never left my side for very long.

For the last 5 years or so, as I've gone through my own processes of growth and transformation, there has been an aspect of the Morrigan to look to for guidance and connection. I trust that She will continue to walk with me every step of the way for the rest of my life. Writing about Her and writing about my process with Her, awakens new levels of devotion inside of me.

I was reflecting the other day on a beautiful dream image I had and began to write a poem. Just like my own personal process with the Morrigan, I didn't know what or who the poem was about until I had finished the first draft. Then it became clear to me.

It was about Her.

Here it is:

Swing-set Over the Moon

Mother,
I would like to see myself in all things.

"Child,
You are everything."

"It is all a lie," She tells
me,
shape-shifting from
a dense mass,
to liquefied light
to a replica
of the Earth.

"I am not what
you think I am."

"I am The Morrigan~
Macha, Badb, Anu, Nemain, Aine, Danu, Raven, Crow, Cattle, Wolf,
Horse, Eel, Swan.

Who are you?"

I am a quiet
girl,
my feet dangling
over the reflection
of a safe night.
I am over the center
of the lake.
How did I get here?
What is the truth?

Why *me?*
Is the moon a small
Earth, or a mirror
for the sun, or made
of dark plastic?

I lean my head to the
right and go to sleep,
relaxing in Her mystery.

"It is in transitions you see most clearly," She whispered.
"Every part of you is natural."

"The part that does not change, ancestral and potent, and the
parts that do, fertility and evolution, will and civilizing art, psychic
and medium, warrior and scavenger, death and liminality,
Sorceress, Lover and Sovereign."

She is all of it,
and in some small way,
so am I,
born to be in awe of Her,
to let her inside,
to show me the fullness
of Being,
to be material for creation.

The Washer at the Ford

Lauren Hershey

They call me the Washer at the Ford.

I stand vigil at the intersection of rivers,
Where you come to cross with clanging swords.
I feel your grim fortune as an icy shiver
And mourn the knowledge I must deliver –
A choice that is meant to be yours.

My disheveled apparition is not a ruse.
I know this news comes freshly laundered for you,
But I have been cleansing it from my mind's long queue.
All the prophetic tribulations and trials anew,
They clang about with kaleidoscopic hues.

Oh, would they just spew out my lips for transparent review.

Is it amusing?
To see what you want to see, to do as you choose?
What freedom must lie in your refusal,
To not know which ends and ways to pursue.
Yet, the clues all lead to the same destination:
Your true path and its cues.

They call me the Washer at the Ford.

I douse the bloody rags of those who seek
Battles before their time, all grim and bleak,
Filled with macabre purpose, no peace to speak.
I beseech you, let this stench reek.

Let its vapors warn others who walk this path
A clarion call for the scavenger's wrath
Hark! Here shall be the last bloodbath.

Here, at the Ford, where harbingers have
Gathered in hopeful mourning,
Shape-shifting Phantastes take flight as a warning.

Visions of raven feathers streak overhead,
Filling you with inspiration or piercing dread,
Calling your heart to act with humility or demanding your head.
Which path do you choose to heed?
Where are you led?

You cannot evade or delay the plucked flower,
Offered to you by the riverside, in the bower.
You cannot ignore spoken truth to power,
In this, your fateful hour.

Oh, how my linens drip with lore and the gore
Of all those who fought for false glory
As I keen and wail with fury.

Pray tell, dear One, what is your hurry?

I am the Morrigan.

I foretell your story.

The Curse of The Morrigan

Lauren Raine

You who bring suffering to children: May you look into the sweetest, most open eyes, and howl the loss of your own innocence.

You who ridicule the poor, the grieving, the lost, the fallen, the inarticulate, the wounded children in grown-up bodies: May you look into each face, and see a mirror. May all your cleverness fall into the abyss of your speechless grief, your secret hunger, may you look into that black hole with no name, and find... the most tender touch in the darkest night, the hand that reaches out. May you take that hand. May you walk all your circles home at last, and coming home, know where you are.

You tree-killers, you wasters – May you breathe the bitter dust, may you thirst, may you walk hungry in the wastelands, the barren places you have made. And when you cannot walk one step further, may you see at your foot a single blade of grass, green, defiantly green. And may you be remade by its generosity.

And those who are greedy in a time of famine: May you be emptied out, may your hearts break not in half, but wide open in a thousand places, and may the waters of the world pour from each crevice, washing you clean.

Those who mistake power for love: May you know true loneliness. And when you think your loneliness will drive you mad, when you know you cannot bear it one more hour, may a line be cast to you, one shining, light woven strand of the Great Web glistening in the dark. And may you hold on for dear life.

Those passive ones, those ones who force others to shape them, and then complain if it's not to your liking: May you find yourself

in the hard place with your back against the wall. And may you
rage, rage until you find your will. And may you learn to shape
yourself.

And you who delight in exploiting others, imagining that you are
better than they are – may you wake up in a strange land as naked
as the day you were born and thrice as raw. May you look into the
eyes of any other soul, in your radiant need and terrible
vulnerability. May you know yourSelf. And may you be blessed by
that communion.

And may you love well, thrice and thrice and thrice,
and again and again and again,
may you find your face before you were born.
And may you drink from deep, deep waters.

Samhain Eve at the River

H. Byron Ballard

Day To Night

It has been a long day
And I am weary.
My feet
     From toe to heel
Ache in my boots.

Let me...
     Ahhhh...
Kick them off and
Spread my body on this moss bed.

The river sings her going song
     A bright time with shadows at the
         Edge.

I sleep
     And dream.
The sun from this long day rises again
And in the shadow world, I relive the whole of it.

Crow and spear point
Blood and grime
I am the Queen of all this: of war and raven.
Mor Righan, Morrighan. More. More.

Waking with eyes shut tight—the lashes
     matted with tears and sweat
And someone's blood—
My ears yearn for the tune in the river.

Motionless I ken it,
     My lips parted as I drink it in.
Coming to my knees—eyes closed to keep in
     The dream-day—
I push myself upright
And lift my hands above me
Imploring the Moon to
     Hold the Night in Her lap
And bed the Day to remain at home

On this last day of the old year,
     This eve of Samhain,
This feast for all the dead.

With my bowl, I scoop the singing waters up
     And pour their songs over
My sore limbs.

Loosing my hair, I comb it with my fingers
     And pour wet music over my head and face,
Over my shoulders and breasts.

Again.
     My soul rises.
I drink the next bowl and it
Sets my mouth for pleasure,
Softens my lips, cleans my throat.

More.
     My hips move stiffly and
I shift my weight so that my feet are apart
From each other, my thighs cooling.

Moonrise

He is a being of sound and chaos
  An Dagda
This wild man who steps with the softness of
A panther.

I hear him as he bursts through
The wood's edge and
  Stops.
He waits, silence covering him,
Clinging to him like mist rising.

I turn my head, craning over my
  Sore shoulder
To watch him. He sets down
His club and the clanging cauldron.

He holds a harp in his
  Large hands and without
His touch, it begins to sing. I turn my body
And face him as he sits by the water.

His fingers on the strings now are
  Deft and sure.
His eyes close to the tenderness
Of the ballad, of his song.

Like a rabbit lured
  To the trap
I step nearer and he sets down
The harp and looks at his hands.

He wrings from my broken body
    A song so dark
And wild that my ears forbid it
Longing instead for a bitter silence.

He pours water over my bitterness
    And presses his lips against
My throat and leads me to
The softness of the moss.

Dawning

Rumble. Gasp. The Sun
    Rises in the roar of his
Snoring. It stops as he reaches out
Straight up toward the sky.

It is the morning of the new year
    And I am hungry as a hunter
Some of the growling in this glen
On this sacred day is my empty belly.

An Dagda sits abruptly and lays his
    Big hands on my belly.
"There is such a hole here—
A hole the size of the Irish Sea!"

He calls the cauldron to his side
    And from it comes sweet honey wine,
Roasted meat and apples, red and gold,
And silver fishes preserved in oil.

He feeds me bite by bite
    The holy foods that honor the dead.
On this first morning of the year. He fills me
With all I desire and then he braids my hair.

War Crow Mixed Media Statue

Molly Roberts

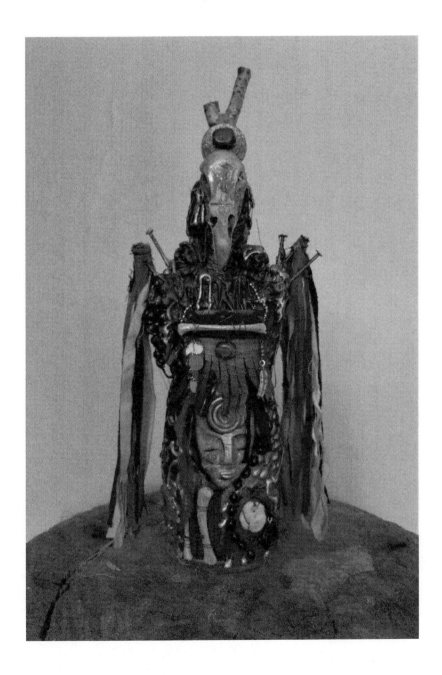

Side view.

Detail, created as a gift for Joey Morris.

The Morrigan Speaks
The Reclamation

Molly Remer

There is a reckoning
and a reclamation
at hand.
The time is now,
the call is loud,
the song is strong.
Reclaim joy,
reclaim your life,
reclaim patience,
reclaim compassion,
reclaim your tenderness
of heart
and fierceness of devotion.
Do not return to apathy
Do not return to complacence,
complicity,
inaction.
Do not go back to sleep.
Resist the fracturing.
Reclaim wholeness
and being here
in your very own life.
Bring awareness into your steps,
your heart,
your choices,
your changes,
your action,
your voice.

Reclaim desire,
reclaim agency,

reclaim your sacred path.
Be present to the unfolding
from within.
Expand into your awakening.

I am the Morrigan
Barbara O' Meara

Warrior Queen Wake-Up Call
Trista Hendren

Dark Goddesses used to frighten me. Most of us are taught to fear them—so as not to get too close to their potency. I was groomed from birth to be a 'good girl,' so reclaiming my power has often been an elusive task.

I was raised with Disney Princesses and bible stories with little mention of women—and certainly not a Warrior Queen who was her own Shero. A Queen implies a woman who is sovereign unto herself—and under the rule of patriarchy, women are anything but.

Mother Mary or a more nurturing Goddess might be more acceptable representations of the washed-down Divine Feminine in the more 'progressive' churches I eventually attended—but *not* The Morrigan. Breaking away *completely* from a fundamentalist Christian background has taken my entire life.

I have come to believe the Dark Goddesses are the last portal to our full humanity—as well as our Divinity.

When I read Iriome R. Martín Alonso's essay in this anthology, it immediately struck a chord. While "being angry and alert" likely saved her from being raped, I felt instantly the stench of the "quietness and submission"[29] doctrine that is still in the air all these years later.

I was never allowed to rage.

Hence I was never able to protect myself. *I froze.*

---

29 "A woman should learn in quietness and full submission."1 Timothy 2:11, NIV. (Paul

As bell hooks wrote, "I was taught as a girl in a patriarchal household that rage was not an appropriate feminine feeling, that it should not only not be expressed but be eradicated."

Suppressing female rage keeps us small, submissive and weak— easy targets. And yet, as Iriome wrote, "acting in cold rage" kept her safe.

This is precisely why 'Good Girls' need The Morrigan. This is absolutely why *everyone* needs The Morrigan. She is calling all of us to wake up—and release ourselves from our cages.

I was conditioned to be frail and to let the men in my life protect and support me.

They rarely did. And some were abusive.

I have played with the idea of taking self-defense classes for several years now, but have never actually signed up for one. While I raised a young knife-throwing Warrioress, I have yet to become one myself—at least physically. Getting back in touch with my body after childhood sexual abuse has been a lifelong process. Andrea Dworkin's transformation sounds completely familiar:

> "I began to know that there was nothing good or romantic or noble in the myths I was living out; that, in fact, the effect of these myths was to deprive me of my bodily integrity, to cripple me creatively, to take me from myself. I began to change in a way so fundamental that there was no longer any place for me in the world—I was no longer a woman as I had been a woman before. I experienced this change as an agony. There was no place for me anywhere in the world. I began to feel anger, rage, bitterness, despair, fury, absolute fury..."

I have come to believe that fury is necessary for those coming out of deeply patriarchal traditions. It is the only way to fully break the chains of oppression.

My transformation has been nearly 30 years in the making. There are always more layers to pull off. The metamorphic effects of experiencing ourselves as Divine cannot be overstated—especially when we are able to embrace ALL of the aspects of Goddess. Starhawk wrote that:

> "The importance of the Goddess symbol for women cannot be over-stressed. The image of the Goddess inspires women to see ourselves as Divine, our bodies as sacred, The Changing Faces of Our Lives as holy, our aggression as healthy, our anger as purifying, and our power to nurture and create, but also to limit and Destroy when necessary, as the very force that sustains all life. Through the goddess, we can discover our strength, Enlighten our minds, own our bodies, and celebrate our emotions, we can move beyond narrow, constricting roles and become whole."[30]

The hardest thing for me to reclaim was healthy aggression and destruction when necessary. As much as patriarchy has been a destructive force in my life, I still have not felt altogether comfortable with taking it down in 'unladylike' ways.

It took me 38 years to be able to yell at my father. At 46, I'm done waiting for the world to change via the peaceful methods most victims are groomed to tolerate. I was tamed to be nice, at all costs—and the price was always mine to pay.

As Deborah A. Meyerriecks wrote earlier in this anthology, "Kind is not always nice and that's OK."

---

30 Starhawk. *The Spiral Dance: A Rebirth of the Ancient Religion of the Goddess.* HarperOne; 20th Anniversary ed. Edition, 1999.

There is nothing nice—or kind—about the state of this world for most of its population. Warrior Goddesses are needed to make our world a kinder place for *everybody*.

It just takes some of us longer to realize that.

I became better familiar with The Morrigan when Jessica Johnson inquired about writing a children's book about Her for our *My Name is* Series[31] several years ago.

I didn't know much about The Morrigan at that time—and She probably was not a Goddess I would have sought out myself, even though I have connected with other Dark Goddesses. In retrospect, this is strange. Although I do have an Irish ancestry, it is my younger sister who has always been more curious about that part of our heritage.

The Morrigan didn't really click with me until I saw Andrea Redmond's crone painting, "The Great Queen."[32]

It was then that I recognized Her immediately. I worked with Her extensively in my late 20's—but She did not reveal Herself as a Goddess. She appeared as a tireless crone in worn out, baggy clothes with a face that always seemed rather bird-like to me.

I began a thorough reprogramming journey in 2002. When I realized I was pregnant with my son, I knew I needed to radically change my dysfunctional default behaviors. Several co-workers were making enormous progress in their lives and they all shared one thing in common: Pat Graves.

---

31 Glenys Livingstone inspired this series with her children's book, *My Name is Medusa*. We now have books on Inanna, Lilith, Isis, The Morrigan and Willendorf—with Brigid and Bouddica in the works.

32 See page 11.

Pat was an unschooled, recovering alcoholic and non-traditional therapist of sorts. Pat was prickly. She was not an easy person and I rarely looked forward to meeting her—although I loved her tremendously. She was a no-nonsense sort of woman, who didn't have the time or patience to be conned. She called you on your shit and she would tell you in no uncertain terms when you were wrong.

Pat changed my life.

When Jessica Johnson wrote about feeling loved by The Morrigan, I knew again exactly what she meant. If it were not for Pat's tough love, I don't know where—or who—I would be today.

I continued moving forward on my self-recovery after my sessions with Pat were over. She provided the tools and the foundation that enabled me to change my life, long after her time on earth was up.

I still tear up when I think about Pat. She was one of the most unique women I have ever known. Her impact on women—and men—in the Portland community was profound. She was extremely humble, so I did not realize how deep her roots were until she left us. Her Memorial Service was packed with person after person who tearfully shared the changes she sparked In their lives. It could have gone on for days.

We need more Pats in this world. We need more of The Morrigan's relentlessness. Most of us are just getting by. The Morrigan challenges us to *really* live. Not to be small. To be our very best selves.

For a long time, I had a photo of Pat up where I could see her every day. When I moved my children to Norway 6 years ago, we brought only 4 suitcases—so there was no room for photos.

With each anthology, I keep something special in my home to remind me of that particular Goddess. This time I know I need to place that photo of Pat on my altar.

I don't know that The Morrigan will ever be my patron Goddess but She has made her mark on me. I like Jean Shinoda Bolen's idea of having Goddess committee members to guide us:

> "In *Goddesses in Everywoman*, I suggested imagining the goddess archetypes as committee members, each speaking for her particular values. Ideally, you should have a well-functioning ego chairing the committee, so that order is maintained, and all perspectives are heard. Knowing which archetypes are active means knowing what is important to you at a given time in your life. It is a way of seeing inner complexity that can lead to understanding inner alliances and conflicts that arise with changing circumstances...
>
> The committee metaphor serves as a shorthand. To call a 'committee meeting' is going inward and 'listening' to the particular archetypes that are active in you. It is a way to make a decision, or find a solution that depends on which archetypes are most important at a given time and resolving inner conflicts and loyalties, before you act. When you pay careful attention and wait for clarity, a choice will emerge that will be right for you. What you do and who you are then coincide."[33]

It occurred to me on Mother's Day that I have often over-identified with the Mother archetype at the expense of myself. Co-dependency has been a lifelong affliction for me. I often over-mother my family and even the world at large. The Morrigan seems the perfect archetype to break that cage wide open.

---

33 Shinoda Bolen, Jean. "Listening to your inner committee." Facebook post on April 30th 2021.

I can't think of a better Goddess to chair my meetings than The Morrigan—or the no-nonsense crone, Pat Graves—whose voice I still often hear in my head when making a decision.

Stephanie Woodfield wrote that:

> "The dark goddess and the lessons she teaches are vital to our lives. Her destructive aspects teach us that there is death within life, that we are constantly changing and evolving. No matter what we have been through in our lives, we can rise from the ashes and like Kali dance ecstatically on the ruins of our old selves toward re-birth. As the fierce warrior drinking the blood of the slain, she is a no-nonsense goddess, teaching us to make our voices heard, to stand up and be counted, and inspiring us to bring about change, both in ourselves and the world around us. And she is also the shadowy keeper of the dead, teaching us how to pierce the veil, to see into the future, and to commune with the beloved dead. But she is also the side of the Divine that we avoid the most, and as a consequence we often have difficulty working with her."[34]

The last 16 months have been a re-birthing process for much of the world. Many claim that the old ways are falling down. I am not certain of that—*yet*. However, there is no doubt that much pain and trauma have been revealed—and some of it has been healed.

We are at a pivotal point going forward. Will we continue to support the status quo—*or will we demand and create an entirely new world?*

The Morrigan is just the Goddess to usher the shift we desperately need. May we give Her the welcome party She deserves.

---

34 Woodfield, Stephanie. *The Dark Goddess Craft: A Journey Through the Heart of Transformation.* Llewellyn Publications; 2017.

List of Contributors

Alissa DeLaFuente lives and works in the Pacific Northwest. Her fiction, nonfiction, and poetry have appeared in scientific and literary journals, including *Gold Man Review*, *Red Savina Review*, and others. In response to the pandemic, she wrote and self-published a book on time management and gentle goal-setting to help young people manage the chaos. It came out in May 2020, and is titled *Get Your Life Together: A practical guide to getting organized*. She regularly serves as a prose judge for the International Latino Book Awards. Visit her at www.alissadelafuente.com to learn more.

Alyssa Spungen (she/her/hers) works in Behavioral Health, is a Yoga teacher and Dream-worker in Tucson, AZ. Alyssa posts magick and dream-related things on Instagram @yourdreamfish.

Andrea Redmond has been a feminist rights activist, artist and pagan for over 50 years. She has been a devotee of The Morrigan since a young girl.

She was born on Prince Edward Island, Canada of Irish descent and moved to Ireland with her young family and there, she was one of the first women in Belfast to paint wall murals. Her first mural in 1983 honoured women's rights activists from Ireland and South Africa. She has painted over 40 murals with similar themes and her work has been featured in a number of publications and films on Northern Ireland.

She has worked and chaired a number of women's, art and multicultural groups. She has taught programs in art, community development and youth work. She is a mother to three children and returned to education in her 40s, completing her PhD, at the University of Ulster.

Andrea currently resides in rural Donegal, Ireland where she operates her art studio/workshop. Her artwork is in permanent collections and galleries in Ireland, Canada and the United States.

Arlene Bailey is a visionary artist and author working in the realm of the Sacred Female in all her many visages. Arlene's paintings and poetry/prose reflect the raw, visceral and sacred wild in all women, while challenging and questioning everything we know to be true about *the who* of who we are as women walking in this time.

Through her magical weavings in word and paint—and, drawing on her trainings and skills as an Ordained Priestess, Women's Mysteries Facilitator, Wise Woman Herbalist, Energy Medicine Practitioner and Retired Anthropologist—Arlene invites women to step into personal sovereignty as they listen to their ancient memories and voice of their soul.

Published in several Girl God Books' anthologies, Arlene is also a monthly contributor to *Return to Mago* E-Magazine and has writings in two forthcoming Mago anthologies. Her work can also be found on *The Sacred Wild*, a page on Facebook about re-wilding woman's soul.

Along with her partner and five cats, this Wild Crone lives on 18 acres of deep woods and quartz outcroppings in the Uwharrie Mountains of North Carolina, USA.

www.facebook.com/sacredwildstudio
www.instagram.com/arlenebaileyartist
www.magobooks.com
www.magoism.net

Arna Baartz is a painter, writer/poet, martial artist, educator and mother to eight fantastic children. She has been expressing herself creatively for more than 40 years and finds it to be her favourite way of exploring her inner being enough to evolve positively in an externally-focused world. Arna's artistic and literary expression is her creative perspective of the stories she observes playing out around her. Claims to fame: Arna has been selected for major art prizes and won a number of awards, published many books, and— (her favourite) was being used as a 'paintbrush' at the age of two by well-known Australian artist John Olsen. Arna lives and works from her bush studio in the Northern Rivers, NSW Australia. Her website is www.artofkundalini.com.

Ashley McCormack, PhD MSW fell in love with poetry when she was in high school, especially sonnets. Something about structure was freeing. After many years in school, she spent 20 years using big machines to explore invisible things and eventually found comfort in mystery and exploration. As a scientist, she contributed to many academic articles and once served as editor for a journal issue on scientific methods. Ashley has been a progressive minister for 22 years, facilitating workshops, officiating rituals, and offering spiritual companionship. Ashley lives in St. Louis and spends her time practicing art, poetry, and divination in the more than human world. She is currently writing a book about Eve and how women create the world in the midst of life. Ashley can be reached at www.ashleylmccormack.com.

Barbara O'Meara is a published writer, co-editor of *Soul Seers Irish Anthology of Celtic Shamanism*, and a professional visual artist.

Exhibitions include 'B.O.R.N. -Babies of Ravaged Nations', group shows Lockhart Gallery New York & 'The Drawing Box' Europe, America, Far East & 'Herstory' Brigid's of the World & Black Lives Matter.

Community projects i.e. 'Stitched With Love' Tuam Baby Blanket laid over the burial site at the Mother & Child Home, shown at KOLO International Women's Non Killing Cross Borders Summit in Sarajevo held by Bosnian women survivors. She is continually developing empowering women's 'Art as Activism' events i.e. 'Sort Our Smears' Campaign at 'Festival of FeminismS'.

Her Collections include: Microsoft, ESB, Dept Foreign Affairs, Irish Life, Impact Trade Union, Bologna District Council, Behaviour & Attitudes.

A recent art review stated: "Barbara O'Meara's recent paintings dealing with home and Covid are extremely beautiful and extremely coherent in their communication. Rarely is it seen where painting is used to convey complex emotional human conditions." www.barbaraomearaartist.com

Barbara Whiterose Marie McSweeney, Ph.D., is a composer, performer, creative writer, and scholar. Her theatrical presentations and concert works engage with Celtic Goddesses and Spirits, such as Macha, Brigid, Cerridwen, and Awenyddion (her own female version of Taliesin). She is also an idiosyncratic clarinetist, exploring the wonders of the sounding breath through a kinship with the solo Zen repertoire of the Japanese bamboo flute. Current composing/performing projects include duos with shakuhachi performer Riley Lee and with Cape Breton guitarist Charles MacDonald. Barbara Whiterose's latest CD, Farewell to Music, is forthcoming on Albany Records. She is grateful to Tom Cowan and Susan McClellan for their teachings in Celtic shamanism. Website: iammakingthisup.com

Through adversity, being a resilient, confident leader, from a woman who employed these skills to conquer early violence and sexual abuse, to leading in the construction world while living with a disability – this is **Bek Paroz** and her story.

Becky Paroz comes from a dysfunctional family. This combined with a chronic incurable disease diagnosis at age 18, led her on the warrior journey to find her power and her true self. She is a qualified performance coach, a highly experienced mentor to women in male dominated industries, a much-requested public speaker and workshop facilitator. She writes regularly for a wide range of global magazines, has contributed to numerous anthologies, and is working on her first fiction novel. She has become the GladiatHER she needed when she was young. Bek supports all women to step up and showcase their skills. You can read more of her tale via www.wordsofbek.com.au.

H. Byron Ballard, BA, MFA, is a western NC native, teacher, folklorist and writer. She has served as a featured speaker and teacher at Sacred Space Conference, Summerland Spirit Festival, Pagan Spirit Gathering, Southeast Wise Women's Herbal Conference, Glastonbury Goddess Conference, Heartland, Sirius Rising, Starwood, Scottish Pagan Federation Conference and other gatherings. She is senior priestess and co-founder of Mother Grove Goddess Temple and the Coalition of Earth Religions/CERES, both in Asheville, NC.

Her essays are featured in several anthologies and she writes a regular column for *Witches and Pagans Magazine*. Her book *Staubs and Ditchwater* debuted in 2012 and the companion volume *Asfidity and Mad-Stones* was published in Oct. 2015. *Embracing Willendorf: A Witch's Way of Loving Your Body to Health and Fitness* launched in May, 2017. "Earth Works: Ceremonies in Tower Time" debuted in June 2018. Byron is currently at work on *Gnarled Talisman: Old Wild Magics of the Motherland* and *The Ragged Wound: Tending the Soul of Appalachia*.

Claire Dorey
Goldsmiths: BA Hons Fine Art.
Main Employment: Journalist and Creative, UK and overseas.
Artist: Most notable group show; Pillow Talk at the Tate Modern. Included in the Pillow Talk Book.

Curator: 3 x grass roots SLWA exhibitions and educational events on the subject of Female Empowerment, showcasing female artists, academic speeches and local musicians. Silence Is Over – Raising awareness on violence towards women; Ex Voto – Existential Mexican Art Therapy; Heo - Female empowerment in the self portrait.

Extra study: Suppressed Female History: History of the Goddess; Accessing Creative Wisdom; Sound and Breath Work; Reiki Master; Colour Therapy; Hand Mudras; Reflexology; Sculpture. Teaching Workshops: Sculpture and Drawing.

Deborah A. Meyerriecks is a retired NYC*EMS Lieutenant from the NYC Fire Department. A self-dedicated Witch and acting community priestess she has offered guidance and spiritual counseling to support others while they discover their own personal right path. Since responding to the Call of The Morrigan and becoming Her priest, she found her self-healing and shadow work have been exponentially more productive as she navigates her personal lessons this life has to offer. Deborah's first manuscript was recently completed and although still in editing, she is excited for the upcoming release of *Macha and the Medic: Service and Priesthood on the Frontlines of Life*.

In her younger days, **Erika Lopp** chose a path to help others. She attended college and received a Bachelor of Arts in Sociology and later a Master's in Education and Counseling Psychology in order to help victims of domestic violence. Later, her heart led her to an Anthropology degree out of her love for history, archaeology, and cultural studies. She currently works for a cultural resource management firm called Corn Island Archaeology. Her passions include an avid love for the realm of magic, including mythology, magical herbalism, and moon lore. Her creative soul has led to a love for gardening, healing herbs, arts, crafts, baking, photography and writing. Things that inspire Erika: An open moonflower at dusk, the sunrise on a cool fall morning, and the distant call of the crow.

Iriome R. Martín Alonso is a Priestess of the Goddess and an anthropology and performing arts student, born in the Canary Islands (Gran Canaria, 1996). Practising over a decade now, she considers being a witch her identity, paganism her religion and being a priestess her vocational job. She works from archetypes, ritual drama, performance, symbol and emotion, with a deep background in traditional European magic as well as academic knowledge. She focuses on endemic spiritualities from her lands, the Canary Islands and the Iberian Peninsula, as well as hellenic, celtic and avalonian deities/spirits, and offers courses, meditations, rites of passage, ceremonies and sacred theatre.

Iris Eve is a poet, singer-songwriter, artist, tarot reader and the founder and curator of "SHE On The Tip Of Her Tongue," a popular social media site that amplifies the voices and art of women. You can find her at cunningandkeening.com.

Iyana Rashil prefers evolutionary lenses to look at life through, saying it moves the past into new insights. Her degree in Human Development grounds her. Interlace this with a love for universal spiritual paths and consciousness curiosities and an Evolutionary Visionary Spiritualist is born. She blogs her perspectives at thenewerview.com and her self-published works are *Amour Desiré: Aphrodite's Dance with the Colors of Higher Love*, *Number Eleven Authentic Numerology Messages* and *Garments of Inner Power*. A planned release this year is *Sister SiStar Sistah*, a book on birthing feminine consciousness and empowerment through core vision and breaking the spell on words. She is included in two anthologies, *Inanna's Ascent: Reclaiming Female Power* and *Kintsugi*.

Jaclyn Cherie has her roots in Upstate New York. She is an Author, Witch, Feminist and Luciferian. The Owner and Creatrix of The Nephilim Rising strives to tell raw, real stories of Magick, the human condition, Sacred Sex, Women's Issues and her favorite topic, rebellion. Preferring the Shadows to the Light, her Magick and writing reflect this; it is in the Darkness that she found her true form. Her written works originate from the watery depths of her Cancerian Soul and chronicle her cyclical death and rebirth from the Womb of the Dragon.

Jessica Johnson is a contemporary witch and tarot reader who has been on the pagan path for about 20 years. She is a mom to 3 active kids and also runs a tarot reading business, Stellar Tarot. Jessica loves to garden, read, write, paint and knit. Her YouTube channel, StellarRainDancer, is dedicated to talking about tarot, witchcraft, shamanism and pagan parenting. Jessica has been a Daughter of The Morrigan for over four years now—and is committed to bringing a modern, fresh take to the pagan community on working with traditionally darker goddesses.

Joey Morris is a Celtic Creatrix and UK-based daughter of The Morrigan. She is an author, creatrix CEO of Starry Eyed Supplies, and co-owner of the What the Flux podcast.

> "To become a tempered blade of The Morrigan, one must be baptized in blood and fire. These struggles within my lifetime have led me to become a voice for the voiceless, to reach out to the broken, and to poke the shadows in others so that they might begin to heal.

> Such a path is dangerous. But so are we. This is the birth of a wild witch who sees with their 'other eyes' and treads the path of edges, sharp and unusual, but filled with adventure, magick of the liminal and the in-between spaces." – Joey Morris

Within the spiritual landscape, her soul mission is to deepen the understanding of our interconnectedness by both honouring the sacred and exploring the masks of the self through channelling relationships to the Divine through written work, poetry, videos, products, and services.

Karen Storminger has been a practicing polytheist pagan most of her life. Her interests and practices include an eclectic mix of paganism, healing practices and personal study and practice with The Morrigan, Hecate, Brigid, and most recently The Cailleach. Karen is a devotee of The Morrigan. She is an active member of the Connecticut Wiccan and Pagan Network and The Tuatha De

Morrigan groups. She has been writing poetry of all kinds since an early age and blogs periodically at https://thecrowandthedragonfly.wordpress.com/

She has had poetry published in anthologies; "Garland of the Goddess" and "The Dark Ones" as well as other written works. Both a teacher and a healer in all aspects of her life, Karen believes that living itself is an act of devotion and walks through each day with the Goddess at her back, by her side and always in her heart.

Karen Ward PhD is a Shamanic Therapist, Supervisor and Teacher. Trained in the Celtic lineage and Druidic traditions, she co-founded and runs the Slí An Chroí School of Irish Celtic Shamanism with her husband John Cantwell. Her very popular Moon Mná (Gaelic for Moon Women), the women's section, offers online courses incorporating Rite of Passage Ceremonies inspired by the archetypal energies of the Irish Goddesses. Karen is author of renowned book *Change a Little to Change a Lot* (2009), co-editor of *Soul Seers – an Irish Anthology of Celtic Shamanism* (2019) and the annual *Moon Mná Diary-Journal* (2017) to date. She is a Counselling Psychotherapist and Supervisor based at her Dublin Clinic since 1997, leading workshops countrywide and abroad to teach her Energy Therapy technique based on Celtic Shamanism to fellow health practitioners. She is honoured to have co-rediscovered the Brigid's Way Celtic Pilgrimage in 2012. www.slianchroi.ie www.moonmna.ie www.drkarenwardtherapist.ie

Kat Shaw prides herself on breaking through the stereotypical views of beauty that have been cast upon society by the media, having made her name painting the glorious reality that is a woman's body.

Her nude studies of real women garnered unprecedented popularity within only a few short months, as women were crying out for themselves to be portrayed in art, rather than the airbrushed images of the perfection of the female form that are so rife in today's culture.

After graduating with a fine art degree, Kat achieved a successful full-time teaching career for 14 years and continues to teach art part-time whilst passionately pursuing her mission of world domination by empowering as many women as possible to reach their fullest potential by embracing their bodies and loving themselves wholeheartedly.

Kat spreads her inspirational magic through her artwork, her Wellbeing business "Fabulously Imperfect," and her dedication to Goddess energy.

Reiki is a huge part of her life, and as a Reiki Master, Kat is committed to sharing Reiki, teaching Usui, Angelic and Karuna Reiki, and channelling Reiki energy through her artwork to uplift and heal.

As a Sister of Avalon, Kat also works directly with her Goddess consciousness, connecting to Goddess and Priestess energy and translating it into Divine Feminine infused paintings to inspire women and spread Goddess love.

Kat is also a bellydancer and an avid pioneer to improve the lives of rescue animals, and mum to a gorgeous teenage daughter.

Kay Turner has been teaching and working with children and adults in a pastoral and healing capacity since 1996. She graduated from Durham University with a BA (hons) First-Class in Theology in 1995 and went on to study a PGCE in Religious Education at York St John the following year.

Kay worked in Secondary Education as a teacher of RE, Psychology and Health and Social Care. She served as a Curriculum Leader and a Sixth Form Head of Year between 1996 and 2016, apart from a short career break during which she gave birth to three children, completed a counselling qualification, earned a MA in Theology and undertook volunteer pastoral work at a Healing Centre.

Since 2016 Kay has qualified as a Wellbeing Coach, Yin Yoga Teacher and a Trainer and Advanced Practitioner in Energy Medicine, Mysticism and Shamanic Healing. She also walks the Priestess Path. Kay works as a Body, Mind & Soul Evolution Practitioner working with clients individually as well as facilitating workshops and retreats. She is an Intuitive, Energy and Shamanic Mentor and Advocate for Sacred Womanhood Growth.

Kerry Purdy is a self-advocate for autism and C-PTSD, as well as a state soldier and search and rescue technician. In her spare time, she enjoys writing, hiking, endurance running, dark yoga, and playing basketball; and she has a shameless stuffed animal collection. She hopes that one day there will be a world where everyone's strengths and talents are acknowledged!

Laura Diane Cameron is a Seattle-based artist and witchy nerd, born and raised in the beautiful Pacific Northwest. She loves the partly-cloudy, temperate climate (with occasional sun break). She received her BFA in Painting from Washington State University and has been creating mixed media visionary paintings for over two decades. Much of her inspiration comes from dreaming, journeying and channeling images of Goddesses, fey creatures and mythical landscapes.

Her projects and commissions have ranged from book illustration, album covers, movie props, portraits of people and animals, interior murals, Oracle decks, and visionary altarpieces for practitioners, empaths and dreamers.

For further inquiries on prints and originals, please visit lauradianecameron.com.

Lauren Hershey is an avid storyteller, writer of speculative fiction and poetry, and an unconventional Plutonian who revels in weaving creativity from the unseen realms into practical everyday use. Since 2012, she has worked in international conflict transformation and peacebuilding, interpersonal conflict resolution, education, and storytelling. Lauren is passionate about equipping individuals and communities with resources for self-discovery and empowerment and tools to navigate and transform conflict narratives with courage and empathy.

Lauren Raine, MFA, has been creating visual and performance art about the Great Mother since the early 80's. She studied sacred mask traditions in Bali, and exhibited at Buka Creati Gallery in Ubud, Bali. Her collection of "contemporary Temple masks" devoted to worldwide stories of the sacred feminine, The Masks of the Goddess, traveled throughout the U.S. for over 20 years used by dancers, ritualists and storytellers. Venues included the Chapel of Sacred Mirrors, the International Mask Symposium, the New College of California, and the Parliament of World Religions. In 2007 she received a Fellowship with the Alden Dow Creativity Center at Northwood University and a Puffin Grant for her "Spider Woman" Community Arts Project. In 2009 she was resident artist at the Henry Luce Center for the Arts at Wesley Theological Seminary in Washington, DC. Currently she works in ceramic sculpture and teaches at the Tucson Clay Co-op. www.laurenraine.com www.masksofthegoddess.com

Lisbeth Cheever-Gessaman is the artist and illustrator of *The Divine Feminine Oracle* and *The Spellcasting Oracle*. She is a scholar of the Divine Feminine, and a visionary artist who merges magick and technology with traditional mediums to create new interpretations of myth and archetype. Through her work she explores shamanic, astrological and mythological constructs to interpret the liminal worlds of the Divine Feminine, incorporating art and talisman to create a third phenomenon, or magical reality.

In honor of the Great Mother, and as personal witness, she creates all work under the pseudonym "SheWhoIsArt."

219

Website: www.shewhoisart.com
Facebook: www.facebook.com/shewhoisart
Instagram: shewhois

Mary Ellen Talley's poems have recently been published in *Raven Chronicles, U City Review* and *Ekphrastic Review* as well as in the anthologies, *All We Can Hold* and *Ice Cream Poems*. Her poetry has received two Pushcart Nominations.

Molly Remer has been gathering the women to circle, sing, celebrate, and share since 2008. She plans and facilitates seasonal retreats and rituals, mother-daughter circles, family ceremonies, and red tent circles in rural Missouri. She is a priestess who holds MSW, M.Div, and D.Min degrees and wrote her dissertation about contemporary priestessing in the U.S. Molly and her husband Mark co-create Story Goddesses, original goddess sculptures, ceremony kits, mini goddesses, and more at Brigid's Grove. Molly is the author of *Womanrunes, Earthprayer, the Goddess Devotional, Sunlight on Cedar, Whole and Holy, She Lives Her Poems, Walking with Persephone* (forthcoming from Womancraft Publishing) and *The Red Tent Resource Kit* and she writes about thealogy, nature, practical priestessing, and the goddess at *Patreon, Brigid's Grove, Feminism and Religion*, and *Sage Woman Magazine.*

brigidsgrove.etsy.com
patreon.com/brigidsgrove

Molly Roberts is a mixed media painter, art witch and author living on the shores of Lake Michigan. Her colorful approach centers on the space where the arts and magickal traditions overlap with a focus on self-discovery and play. Over the past seven years, Molly's work has inspired burgeoning artists all over the world to create art and magick in their own lives through her YouTube channel, books and online community.

Nicola O'Hanlon is an Irish writer of essays and poetry on Feminism, Civil Rights, Mental Health and Addiction. She has a background in Holistic Health practices and care of the elderly. She lives with her partner, two children and an array of cats and dogs on the southeast coast of Ireland in a farmhouse behind tall trees.

Nikki Wardwell Sleath, MA, a direct descendant of one of the colonial citizens of Salem accused and killed for Witchcraft, is a lifelong witch herself. Originally a physical therapist by trade, her foray into integrative health and healing and her spiritual practice and formal training as a witch have led her to a long-term, full-time career teaching magick in her order, the Society of Witchcraft and Old Magick. She is a healer, hypnotherapist, dreamwork facilitator, author, wife and a mom to two wonderful teenagers. She has also been a teacher and priestess serving at the annual Morrigan's Call Retreat for several years. All of these aspects of her life have been made more fulfilling by her devotion to the Great Queen, An Morrioghain.

Pat Daly (editor) is a mother of three daughters and proud grandma. A published author / writer on career and job search issues, Pat lives in Portland, Oregon.

Born in Dublin Ireland, **Paul Nixon** has been creating art for the past nineteen years, but his passion for woodworking began in his early childhood. Surrounded by a family of cabinet makers Paul quickly took on the family skills. Paul spent much of his early childhood with his grandparents in the mountains of County Sligo in northwest Ireland. Paul's grandmother Margaret had a great influence over him. She spent a good deal of her 83 years living on these slopes and its wild glaciated lands where she was tuned into the historical, mystical, and legendary wonders that enveloped this area. Margaret endeared Paul with these qualities which allowed his imagination to evolve and develop the skills that would serve him well in later years.

Working in 3-dimensional works allowed Paul's skills to expand into painting, stained glass, cement and resin casting and photography. Several of his bronze public sculptures adorn the city of Greensboro and the surrounding area as well as liturgical carvings across the USA and Ireland. His photography and his carved fairies caught the attention of the William Butler Yeats Society in New York and Ireland. Last year he was invited to NYU to be involved in a tribute celebrating WB Yeats where he provided a PowerPoint presentation of his work and its relation to the works of Yeats.

As an artist/sculptor/ photographer Paul has been accused of being a bit of a chameleon with his subject matter and style running the gamut from Contemporary/Abstract to Classical Renaissance. He is a visionary who is talented in many mediums and is constantly savoring the excitement of exploration and experimentation. In the 22 years living in Greensboro, North Carolina, Paul has carved out a reputation as an artist, sculptor and photographer.

Phoenix Angelis, Celtic Nocturnal Witch, has been a practitioner of the Craft for the past 20 years. Though her path has changed over time, it has been a constant source of strength. Narrowing to a more Celtic-centric path in the last six years—The Morrigan's call a more recent shift. Being born with Stage I Cerebral Palsy has given her a unique perspective and shown her what strength and resilience truly mean. Phoenix stands with those who are voiceless, those who struggle: Animals, the disabled, LGBTQ+, BIPOC, and all those who are marginalized.

Hot mess, turned emblazoned oracle, **Raya Elyse Bencivenga** is no stranger to the contrast of embodying her divine nature. Equal parts earth mother and wounded healer, Raya blends her lived experiences with intuitive insight as she articulates the complexities of the human condition.

She is an artist, singer-songwriter, poet, energy healer, channel, psychic medium, and tarot professional living in Northern Alberta, Canada with her partner, son, and their rescue dog.

Rosanna Maria Maher is an artist, caregiver, and activist who grew up in New York City. She attended School of the Museum of Fine Arts, Boston. She has worked as a professional dyer for stage and film costuming, an environmental educator for children, a DJ for a pan-Celtic radio show, and a roving craftsperson. Her relationship with the Morrigan has deepened during the decade of caregiving for her mother who has dementia, and through activist work addressing systemic trauma. Rosanna enjoys practicing permaculture in her bioregion, walking hounds, archery, roses and thorned plants, traveling, and healing work with horses. See RoseThornCollective on Etsy. She spends her time engaged between NYC and the wild coast of New England.

For nearly 5 years, **Sam (Bo) Thompson** has been bound to The Morrigan and is now embracing (read that as pushed into) the role as Her Priest. He says, 'the last half decade has been a whirlwind with Herself and has felt a bit like drinking from a firehose most of the time. And I would not change a thing!' A big part of his work with The Morrigan is blacksmithing. He considers himself a magical blacksmith and enjoys bringing magic into his sacred forge work. It brings him a deep delight to co-create metalwork for people, both for their magical working, and items that can easily become heirloom pieces. Several times a year, he hosts weekend primitive blacksmithing intensives and magical blacksmithing weekends at Ravens Keep Forge located on the land he caretakes, Shadow Sanctuary in NC.

Sharon Smith is a writer, ghost writer, editor, and proofreader with a passion for helping women reconnect with their Authentic Selves and Voices. She loves and honors the Great Mother in all Her many forms, and has a deep connection to Nature. She identifies as a Green Witch and follows an eclectic spiritual path that is a blending of Native American and Celtic Teachings, both in her ancestral line.

Sionainn McLean is a polytheist fire witch, on a crazy spiritual journey over the last 25 years. She has worked with The Morrigan for 5+ years. She is currently studying to get her certificate in Community Ministry, as well as a Spiritual Direction certificate with Cherry Hill Seminary. She is also studying magic and shamanistic practice with Three Worlds, One Heart School of Mystery. She's also a mom, wife, writer, and gardener.

Stephanie Woodfield (Orlando, FL) has been a practicing Pagan for the past twenty years. A devotional polytheist, teacher, and Priestess of the Morrigan, she is one of the founding members of Morrigu's Daughters and is an organizer for several Pagan gatherings. Stephanie teaches classes on devotional work and magical practice in the US and internationally. A long time New Englander, she now resides in the Orlando area with her husband, a very pampered cat, and various reptiles. In her spare time, she enjoys creating art out of skulls and other dead things. She is called to helping others forge meaningful experiences with the Morrigan, as well as the Gods and land of Ireland. Visit her online at https://www.stephaniewoodfield.com

Teresa Hess lives on an island in the Salish Sea with her husband and three daughters, where they live an unschooling life together. Teresa loves to play with her kids, be outside, swim in the Puget Sound, dance her heart out, write about her internal process, learn from her emotions, act, sing, laugh, breathe, make delicious food, and watch shows with her family. More of her writing can be found on her blog, https://sparkleandzest.com/ or on Instagram @sparkleandzest.

Trista Hendren founded Girl God Books in 2011 to support a necessary unraveling of the patriarchal world view of divinity. Her first book—*The Girl God*, a children's picture book—was a response to her own daughter's inability to see herself reflected in God. Since then, she has published more than 25 books by a dozen women from across the globe. Originally from Portland, Oregon, she now lives in Bergen, Norway with her family. You can learn more about her projects at www.thegirlgod.com.

Trista's Acknowledgments

I would like to acknowledge my co-editors. My mother, **Pat Daly,** has edited each and every one of my books. There would be no Girl God Books without her many contributions. I was thrilled to also work with **Jessica Johnson** again on this project—who inspired my interest in The Morrigan.

Tremendous gratitude to **Arna Baartz** for being a part of this project from the beginning and allowing us to feature her gorgeous painting as the cover art.

Many thanks to **Joey Morris** for writing the beautiful Preface to this anthology.

Many thanks (and so my love) to my talented son, **Joey Hopkins,** who designed the cover and sends out book orders. Also to my daughter **Helani Claire** for her constant inspiration.

Appreciation to my beloved husband **Anders Løberg**, who prepared the document for printing and helped with website updates. Your love, support and many contributions made this book possible.

My mom and I would also like to acknowledge her wonderful partner, **Rick Weiss,** for being an all-around awesome guy—and helping us with the page numbers.

Special thanks to my sister and fellow-contributor **Sharon Smith** for giving me feedback on my piece and her all-around cheery helpfulness.

Lastly, I would like to thank my dear sisters **Tamara Albanna, Monette Chilson, Monica Rodgers** and **Alyscia Cunningham** for always being right there to cheer me on in the spirit of true sisterhood.

Thank you to all our readers and Girl God supporters over the years. We love and appreciate you!

Jessica's Acknowledgments

First and foremost, I want to thank my husband Neil for his patience, his love, belief in me, and his tolerance of me. I'm opinionated, a fierce feminist, environmentalist, and believer in fighting for social justice and rights amongst marginalized people, and to most men, that would be a huge turn off. Somehow you managed to see past all that to the vulnerable creature that I am, and have loved me anyways. I'm proud to call you my partner in life (and in crime, though really, let's be honest, our crimes are few and boring) and to raise our children together with you.

To my children, I can't call you anything less than my greatest teachers. This last year or so has been so hard for you, cut off from friendships and normal life, and you have not only survived it, you've taught me so much about how to thrive under these conditions. I won't lie, you drive me crazy at times, but ultimately my love for you is what gets me out of my bed in the morning, and I would do just about anything to make sure you all feel loved and accepted. Morgan, I can't believe how amazing our relationship has become in the past couple of years and I can't wait to see what kind of adult you'll become. You astound me with your emotional intelligence, and I hope that one day I can be as confident as you are around other people. Your ability to make friends is enviable! Andrew, I don't know how you build the things you do, but keep on doing it. If you're not somehow designing the way we live our lives or the buildings we see in public one day, I'll eat my shirt. Don't ever let other people tell you that being sensitive is a bad thing, because it's a gift. Also, you give darn good hugs. Emelie, you are so very trying at times, but I know that this fierce little girl is one day going to make waves in the world. It's a darn good thing you're still in grade school, because the world isn't ready for you yet. Your spirit is inspiring, and you make me laugh just as much as you make me want to scream.

My mother and father, my now late in-laws and my supportive family members and chosen family – thank you to all of you who have believed in me and supported me. I know I'm a kooky one, and not always the easiest to get along with or love, but I am grateful for your support as I've chased my dreams. I especially want to say thank you to my Grandma who fed my love of being creative. I can only imagine how relieved you were when I finally want to bed every night at Kelly Lake, but I want you to know that I cherish those memories, and I think the mark you made on me creatively is the reason that I was able to bring my books into the world. Thank you.

If you enjoyed this book, please consider writing a brief review on Amazon and/or Goodreads.

What's Next?!

The next anthologies in this series are:

In Defiance of Oppression – The Legacy of Boadicea – Edited by Trista Hendren, Joey Morris and Pat Daly

Just as I Am: Hymns Affirming the Divine Female – Edited by Trista Hendren, Sharon Smith and Pat Daly

Re-Membering with Goddess: Healing the Patriarchal Perpetuation of Trauma. – Edited by Kay Turner, Trista Hendren and Pat Daly.

Lotus Heart: The Compassion of Kuan Yin – Edited by Trista Hendren, Herng Yu Tzong, and Yeshe Matthews

The Crone Initiation and Invitation: Women speak on the Menopause Journey – Edited by Kay Turner, Trista Hendren and Pat Daly

Anthologies and children's books on the Black Madonna, Mary Magdalene, Mother Mary, Aradia, Kali, Brigid, Sophia, Spider Woman, Persephone and Hecate are also in the works.

Details to be announced.

http://thegirlgod.com/publishing.php

Made in the USA
Columbia, SC
29 June 2021